INSPIRATIONAL DEVOTIONS OF HOPE DURING AMERICA'S-COVID PANDEMIC

Leda Rafter

Author's Tranquility Press
MARIETTA, GEORGIA

Copyright © 2022 by Leda Rafter

All rights reserved. No part of this publication may be reproduced, distributed or transmitted in any form or by any means, including photocopying, recording, or other electronic or mechanical methods, without the prior written permission of the publisher, except in the case of brief quotations embodied in critical reviews and certain other noncommercial uses permitted by copyright law. For permission requests, write to the publisher, addressed "Attention: Permissions Coordinator," at the address below.

Leda Rafter/Author's Tranquility Press
2706 Station Club Drive SW
Marietta, GA 30060
www.authorstranquilitypress.com

Ordering Information:
Quantity sales. Special discounts are available on quantity purchases by corporations, associations, and others. For details, contact the "Special Sales Department" at the address above.

Inspirational Devotions of Hope
During America's-Covid Pandemic/Leda Rafter
Paperback: 978-1-959453-64-2
ebook: 978-1-959453-65-9

Scripture quotations marked KJV are from the Holy Bible, King James Version (Authorized Version). First published in 1611. Quoted from the KJV Classic Reference Bible, Copyright © 1983 by The Zondervan Corporation.

DEDICATION

By: Leda Rafter

The book Inspirational Devotions of Hope During America's Covid-Pandemic is dedicated to all the people that have lost their lives due to Covid. The families that have endured the loss of loved ones are in my prayers and thoughts daily. I have faced the loss of children in my own life ....it is a pain that permeates the heart and soul daily as we learn to cope with the sting that death often brings.

I also dedicate Inspirational Devotions of Hope During Americas Covid-Pandemic to my Lord and Savior that has walked with me daily during the good times and the challenging times. He is my hope and anchor as I do life together with him. I can see his handy work in my life as I have learned over the years to trust and have faith while making my journey.

May God Bless you and bless this great Nation that we live in.

Leda Rafter

FOREWORD

By: MyLinda Solley

My cart squeaked as I pushed it past the empty grocery store shelves. Just a few months ago these same shelves were overflowing. People's eyes darted, as not one person seemed to want to make eye contact with me and by isle three, I was in tears. I began to cry as I saw fear on faces as terror gripped people's heart. I started to pray. I knew scripture says over three hundred times to fear not and do not fear.... but here we were in 2020 and God's people forgot.

My Leda did not forget. When the world seemed to spiral into the abyss of fear, she embraced God's confidence (Hebrews 10:23) and as people fell into despair, she grabbed hold of God's hope (Jeremiah 29:11). Leda has had a life filled with challenges, unimaginable loss, and extreme difficulties but you would not know this from casually talking to her. She has an amazing smile that she couples with words of encouragement that brings Christ's light into the world around her, wherever her path leads her. She has learned the secret.

The secret she has learned is not to be tossed back and forth based on current events around her, including a global pandemic. No matter how chaotic the world, she grabs hold of God's plumb line of truth and stays unwavering. God is like her thermostat-constant-no matter what the temperature is outside, her temperature is set. She is not a thermometer that goes up and down based on circumstances. She hangs onto the hope of what she does not yet see because of what God's word says is true (Hebrews 11: 1).

The devotions contained in these pages will dispense wisdom into your life and infuse much needed HOPE. Reading them is like receiving a blessed gift from the wordsmith Leda Rafter. She is my friend and most importantly God's.

MyLinda Solley, RN

Contents

DEDICATION i
FOREWORD iii
HAPPY NEW YEAR 1
BUTTERFLY WITH A BROKEN WING 2
HOPE AND PEACE FOR A NEW YEAR 3
HE IS THE GREAT SHEPHERD 4
A SHELTER IN THE MIDST OF A STORM 5
THE FISHING MIRACLE 6
FAMILY TIME 7
RUNNING THE RACE 8
GOD HAS A PLAN FOR YOUR LIFE 9
LEARNING TO FORGIVE 10
LOVE POURED OUT BY A NURSE 11
LORD SAVE ME I AM DROWNING 12
GETTING RID OF CHILD LIKE BEHAVIOR 13
THE GREAT LOVE STORY WITH JESUS 14
BALM IN GILEAD 15
CAST YOUR CARES ON HIM 16
SEEKING THE GOOD FOR OTHERS 17
WORDS OF WISDOM 18
HOPE FOR FALLEN MANKIND 19
RUN AWAY PROPHET 20
INDIGNANT WORDS 21

ANGELS ALL AROUND..22
HUMILITY 24
INTEGRITY NEVER WAVERING................................25
DIVINE STRENGTH 26
I BELIEVE 27
GOD IS THE GREAT HEALER 28
BLESSINGS OF HOPE 29
EVANGELICAL CHRISTIANS....................................30
MY SPECIAL TIME...31
ALBUQUERQUE NEED..32
MY FRIEND BROTHER KLINE 33
CARING ENOUGH TO SERVE...................................34
A BAG OF PENNIES...35
MR TRACK MAN..36
RED SEA EXPERIENCE..37
WHAT CAN WE DO FOR GOD? 38
THE LORD LOVES A TRUTHFUL TONGUE.............39
WHEN THE WINDS BLOW 40
JESUS LOVES ME THIS I KNOW...............................41
THE ELECTRICAL FENCE 42
NEVER LET YOUR DREAMS DIE 43
SWEET PATRIA..44
COME BACK TO THE FATHER'S HOUSE 45
OTHER PEOPLE'S OPINIONS CANNOT BE MY REALITY 46
SUSTAINING GRACE...47
GOD'S LITTLE ONE...48
LOVE LIFTED ME..49

WE CAN MAKE A DIFFERENCE	50
FINDING MY WAY HOME	51
LIVING WATERS	52
A MOUNTAIN TO CLIMB	53
DO NOT MARK THEM OFF	54
JUMP IN FIRST ASK GOD FOR A BAIL OUT	55
GOD SENT THE QUAIL	56
WHEN YOU PRAY	57
JOY IN A DIVERSE CRISIS	58
THE PAINT BUCKET	59
COME TO MY TABLE	60
JEALOUSY WILL DIVIDE	61
A MARK OF DISTINCTION	62
I WILL NOT SLUMBER OR SLEEP	63
WHAT IS TRUE COMMITMENT	64
HAPPINESS IS A CHOICE	65
GOD CARES ABOUT THE LITTLE THINGS	66
WHAT GIFT WILL I LEAVE FOR CHRIST	67
AMERICA HOLD ON TO YOUR BIRTHRIGHT	68
AMERICA RETURNS TO GOD	69
THE WEDDING FEAST	70
FACING THE GIANTS IN OUR LIVES	71
FAITH WITHOUT QUESTION	72
GOD WILL RESTORE OUR CHILDREN	73
BREATH LIFE INTO THE DRY BONES	74
AMERICA'S PLUM LINE	75
JUST SAY YES	76

WEAKNESS FADES IN THE PRESENCE OF GOD	77
CARRYING THE TORCH OF FAITH	78
A TRIBUTE TO LORETTA LYNN	79
INCREDIBLE FAITH	80
GOD LOVES AMERICA	81
STANDING FIRM	82
EATING AT GOD'S TABLE	83
PRAYER CAN MOVE MOUNTAINS	84
OPPOSITION CANNOT DESTROY YOUR DREAM	85
WAITING UPON GOD	86
MANEUVERING THROUGH THE QUICKSAND	87
OVERCOMING OBSTACLES	88
A FLICKER OF LIGHT	89
TURBULENT WATERS	90
DO NOT LET TROUBLE FRAGMENT YOUR FAITH	91
PALPABLE LOVE	92
GOD WENT BEFORE ME	93
LET'S EAT BREAD TOGETHER	94
WHO DO YOU SAY I AM	95
YOU ATE AND HAD YOUR FILL	96
FRINGE BENEFITS	97
FORFEITING YOUR MIRACLE	98
GIVING BRINGS BLESSINGS	99
UNITY BRINGS STRENGTH TO AMERICA	100
THERE IS A LIGHT THAT SHINES IN THE DARK	101
REJOICING DURING OUR SUFFERING	102
WHEN WE RUN OUT OF OPTIONS	103

MAUNDY FOOT WASHING	104
HE TOUCHED THE COFFIN	105
THE TALKING DONKEY	106
THE WELL OF LIVING WATER	107
OUR RESURRECTED LORD	108
ENDURANCE BRINGS ETERNAL BLISS	109
DELIVERANCE AND PEACE	110
JESUS PICKED THE OBJECTIONABLE	111
MY ANCHOR HOLDS	112
TRIALS RUBBISH COMPARED TO OUR REWARDS	113
JOSHUA'S COMMITMENT	114
GOD WANTS HIS SPECIAL TIME	115
SCARS ARE A SIGN OF HEALING	116
ANGELAS DEFINITION OF FAITH	117
THE JEWISH NAPKIN	118
GOD CHOSE YOU TO WORK FOR HIS CAUSE	119
A SECOND CHANCE AT LIFE	120
AMERICA'S JOURNEY BACK HOME	121
MISSED OPPORTUNITY	122
EVERLASTING LOVE	123
AMERICA WE ARE WEAK BUT YET STRONG	124
MERCY SPILLED OUT	125
WHEN THE WINDS BLOW	126
FOOTPRINTS IN THE SAND	127
THE FALL OF JERICHO	128
THE TRUE VINE BRINGS LIFE TO ALL	129
WHEN A FATHER LOVED ENOUGH TO INSTRUCT	130

SALT OF THE EARTH	131
LOSS OF SLEEP	132
IF WE COULD HAVE A DO OVER	133
A PARENTS DELIGHT	134
A COVENANT WITH OUR LORD	135
A CROSS FOR A BROKEN WORLD	136
AMERICA STANDS WITH YOU UKRAINE	137
WISDOM PREVENTS TRAGEDY	138
JESUS A FRIEND OF THE SINNERS	139
RETURN TO SENDER	140
DIVINE FORGIVENESS	141
HONOR THE DIGNITY OF OTHERS	142
SEEKING COUNSEL	143
A QUIET PLACE OF REST	144
FILL OUR HEARTS WITH NEW WINE	145
QUITTING IS NOT AN OPTION	146
SPREAD THE GOOD NEWS	147
OUR LORD WEPT THREE TIMES	148
SPIRITUAL AWAKENING	149
LET THE WEAK SAY I AM STRONG	150
LITTLE IS MUCH WHEN GOD IS IN IT	151
WAR CRY FROM GOD'S PEOPLE	152
WORDS OF AFFIRMATION	153
I WANT TO GO WITH YOU	154
GOD USES THE INEVITABLE	155
REBUILDING AMERICA	156
A FRIEND OF THE SINNERS	157

JESUS COMMANDED	158
SUBSTAINING THE WEARY	159
LEARN HOW TO BE CHILDLIKE	160
LEAVING HER PAST BEHIND	161
CIRCLE OF LOVE	162
A COMMANDMENT WITH A PROMISE	163
UNIQUELY MADE FOR GOD'S PURPOSE	164
GOD'S PLAN FOR HIS PEOPLE	165
FINE OIL OF PROTECTION	166
THE WISDOM OF DEBORAH	167
THE BUDDED STAFF	168
JESUS DEPLORED RELIGIOUS SYSTEMS	169
A MIRACLE AWAITS AMERICA	170
NEVER LET GO OF YOUR INNER CHILD	171
YOU HAVE A PROMISE LAND	172
ARE YOU THIRSTY?	173
HEALING FOR AMERICA	174
ASK, SEEK, KNOCK	175
AMERICA THE BEAUTIFUL	176
A PARENT'S MIRACLE	177
THE GREATEST MIRACLE IN HISTORY	178
I CAME TO BRING HEALING TO THE SICK	179
HELPING THE WEAK	180
WHERE DO WE GO FROM HERE AMERICA?	181
I KNOW HIM, I CAN FEEL HIM, I CAN SEE HIM	182
ABOUT THE AUTHOR	183

HAPPY NEW YEAR

ISAIAH 43:1-2

When you walk through the fire, you will not be burned; the flames will not set you ablaze. I am the Lord your God the Holy one of Israel, your Savior.

Happy New Year to you as you read this devotion. Our nation is faced with the greatest pandemic with hundreds and thousands of people dyeing daily as we face the challenges to bring healing to our great nation. Overtures put in place by scientist to try and put an end to this deadly virus called Covid.

The word Hope means a feeling of expectation and desire for a certain thing to happen. The scripture in Isaiah gives hope saying that when you walk through the fire, you will not be burned, the flames will not set you ablaze. God's word is forever true. America has faced great challenges leaving many hopeless trying to make sense out of the pandemic.

Life sometimes sends curve balls that leave us feeling helpless and alone. I have had that experience in my own life. The loss of children broke my heart. I felt as if God had gone away. He came to me in the midnight hours giving me hope and healing to my wounded soul. I do not understand why this had to happened, but I do know that God was my Great Shepherd. He gave me sustaining Grace and Mercy through my pain. He will do the same America as we face the challenges ahead. Look up my friend there is Joy in the morning. When we walk through the fire we will not be burned. He is the great God of the universe bringing healing and refuge to the soul.

BUTTERFLY WITH A BROKEN WING

Psalm 34:18

The Lord is close to the brokenhearted and saves those who are crushed in spirit.

Amish country in Ohio has so many beautiful attractions. As I got out of the car, I looked down on the ground. A beautiful butterfly with radiant colors caught my eye. The blues and yellows and some green gave you a display of the rainbow. The problem with the little butterfly it just sat on the ground. I reached down to see if it would move and after a close look, I realized that the little butterfly had a broken wing. I gently picked up the ray of beauty and placed it in a beautiful flowerpot next to the entrance. I went into the store and as I came out, the little masterpiece was still sitting in a beautiful flower pod decorated with natures beautiful colors of pinks, greens, and yellows.

Sometimes as Christians, we go through moments that our wings are clipped and broken. Someone has surfaced an old wound that has hurt the heart so badly that we feel there is no flower pod for the heart to rest. It is a prayer that you have been earnestly praying for that God has not answered yet leaving your spirit broken. Psalm 34: 18. The Lord is close to the brokenhearted and saves those who are crushed in spirit.

Promises from the Lord are forever true. Waiting is the hard part, and essential for healing our brokenness. God takes our broken spirit and places us in a beautiful garden of hope even in the mist of America's Covid pandemic.

HOPE AND PEACE
FOR A NEW YEAR

Acts: 20:28

Keep watch over yourselves and all the flock of which the Holy Spirit has made you overseers. Be Shepherds of the Church of God which he bought with his blood.

As I walked into the church that my parents raised me as an adolescent and teenager, the church had been sold and new membership occupied the building. I sat down at the back of the church as nostalgia filled my mind with Marriage, baptism of myself and children. I could hear an echo with the voice of my little 3-year-old not sure what baptism meant put his own meaning to the occasion as he said loudly, "look mom they dunked him."

The church headquarters was out of California called Living Streams Ministry. A young man by Watchman Nee born in 1903 felt his call to ministry at the age of seventeen. He had a unique gift to pastor and minister to the body of Christ. In 1952 he was imprisoned for his faith. He remained in prison until his death in 1972. From 1922-1950 Nee taught the word of God preaching to people, holding conferences, and conducting training. After the takeover of China, he was arrested for the sake of the gospel. His work still permeates the hearts of the saints of God.

As I left the building that day my mind took me back to the faithfulness of Reverend Nee walking through the prison wall for the cause of his faith. A deep commitment was the anchor that held him when life became hard. Our world can do this too as we walk through the challenging times in America and our nation.

HE IS THE GREAT SHEPHERD

PSALM 23:

Christmas at the small church in Newport News Virginia was so special to children. My part in this program was to say the verse The Lord is My Shepherd, and I shall not want.

I was a young child of four and had difficulty putting to memory this short verse. As they called my name to resight the verse, I quickly ran up front climbing over the alter as if the steps were not there. I echoed the verse; The Lord is my shepherd and that is enough. The memory is still vivid today in my Christian life. God had a purpose for this divine verse for years to come.

When I lost my son at the age of twenty-three, uncontrollable pain filled my heart. Through the scrim of memory, I could see the great shepherd holding my heart in his hand to bring comfort to my soul.

Several years later, my daughter Trina was diagnosed with metastatic breast cancer. The outcome was very painful as I walked through those long hours of radiation and chemotherapy. She passed to the other side to be with our Lord and Savior in 2016. Again, that great scripture that I learned at the age of four brought comfort to a broken heart.

The Lord is my Shepherd and that is ENUFF gave me the sustaining faith that I needed as I walked through my grief. As you take the challenges for today, remember he is your shepherd and will never leave you.

A SHELTER IN THE MIDST OF A STORM

Psalm 91:1

He who dwells in the shelter of the Highest will rest in the shadow of the almighty.

As I looked out the basement door of our home in Birmingham Ohio, a horrendous storm had embarked upon our city. Lightning flashed bringing light to the darkness of our living quarters. As a fifth grader, with each flash I would hold my hands over my eyes slightly peeking through my fingers with anticipation hoping it was safe and the storm was over.

We as Christians have those spiritual storms that come our way. It may be with our children, finances, health issues, our place of employment or a neighbor. In the first chapter of Peter, he gave the Christians that were being persecuted for their faith an antidote for the sinful world that we live in. It was not a peak through the fingers bandage it was true instructions how to shelter our hearts in the center of the highest God when challenges of life encompass our souls.

As you face the challenges that our country is going through today, let the lightning flashes go never peeking through your fingers. Let God give you hope and peace in the mist of this great pandemic, Peter told the Christians GRACE AND PEACE BE YOURS IN ABUNDANCE. 1st Peter 2

THE FISHING MIRACLE

Luke 5:5

Describes the miracle and the faith that Peter had in Jesus. I can envision Peter as he looked out over the sea just hoping for a net full of fish. The waters seemed so empty leaving Peter with such despair. At lake of Gennesaret, Jesus saw two boats left by fishers. As he got into the boat belonging to Simon Peter, he sat down and instructed the people. I can just imagine how Peter must have felt knowing he had worked all night and caught no fish and now Jesus was using his boat for a platform to instruct the people.

When Jesus had finished his teaching, he instructed Peter to pull his boat into the deep waters. Simons words to Jesus, master we have worked all night and have not caught anything but because you say so, I will let down the net. When Peter let his net down, there was so many fish that the net began to break. Jesus had a twofold mission here at lake Gennesaret. He instructed the people and gave Peter a lesson of faith.

My great grandson while visiting me, brough his fishing pole. I have a pond in the back of my home that is a fish and pitch pond. Parkers words after fishing for a while said. "Nana, I just want to catch one fish." The fishing miracle came to mind. I told Parker lets bow our heads and ask God to send you a fish. The prayer was like this. Dear God, please send Parker a fish.

The marshmallows that he used for bait sent many fish his way. As I looked around no one at the pond was catching fish except Parker. God gives us these moments just to let us know that he hears every prayer even the simple ones that so often exemplifies his name. It is yours for the asking.

FAMILY TIME

Family time is such a wonderful time to fellowship and simply catch up. Many years ago, Sunday was always Family time. Mother and Dad would take us for a drive, go for ice cream or just simply stay at home and spend time together. My father played the guitar, and he would gather us together and we would sing our hearts out. That was quality time together as a family unit.

As we look at the family of today, text messaging eliminates interpersonal connections to just a few words. Video's plays havoc with the minds of children. It is just as if we have taken a pacifier plugged it in as our children cry out for family time. Covid is an opportunity that we can bond together as a family unit leaving aside the item that has enslaved families.

The year 2020-2022 has been a year that has rocked the constitution of our country. COVID has hurt the very heart of the people within the United States of America and abroad. Hundreds and thousands of people have died during this pandemic. The families have been forced to stay safe and often staying within the walls of their own home.

In first John 3:11 This is a message you heard from the beginning to love one another. John 3: 1 How great is the love the father has lavished on us that we should be called the children of God. During this Pandemic in our country God has given us a chance to spend time with him. We are part of the family of God and family time without interruption is essential.

RUNNING THE RACE

We live in a country that is faced with a generational gap. Abraham faced that generational gap in the Old Testament. We as parents face the same the dilemma today. We must be vigilant and search out our hearts before almighty God teaching our children the values of our ancestors.

First Corinthians 9:24 Do you not know that in a race all the runners run but only one gets the prize. Run in such a way to get the prize.

When I was about to go into the fifth grade, I saw my mother leave the home and was curious as to where she was going. I walked behind her hoping that she would not turn around and discover that I was following her. In a childlike mind, I just wanted to see where she was going. Children within the neighborhood always called this place the desert. Mother ventured down a little knoll and bowed down on her knees near a tree. She began to pray the most fervent prayer even to this day still takes resident within my heart. She prayed for the redeeming grace for her children and the chaotic world that we lived in. It was those prayers that I heard that gave me the tools to work with as I raised my own family.

Mothers race to throw out the dirt leaving the generational gap behind was imperative. 1 Corinthians 9:26 says, "Therefore I do not run like a man running aimlessly." Running consistently never being disqualified gave her four children that loves the Lord and carries her legacy to this day. As we parent face the challenges that Covid and war brings, may we search God's word throwing out the dirt that the world sometimes offers and fill our children with hope and peace.

GOD HAS A PLAN FOR YOUR LIFE

Jeremiah 29:11

For I know the plans I have for you says the Lord, plans for welfare and not for evil, to you a future and hope.

There have been times in my life when I wanted things my way not thinking of the ramifications of my decisions. As hard as I tried, I would always say, I want it my way.

There is something that God instills within the believer that will beep the soul like a text message warning that the path we are about to take is a no trespassing zone. As I contemplated taking a new job with many benefits that I currently did not have, the job was something that I wanted. The benefits were great and there was no way that the beep within my soul should be sending an alarm saying NO THIS IS A ZONE YOU DO NOT NEED TO ENTER! I reviewed all the options carefully dialogued with the administrator and the staff looking for areas that would constitute the earlier red zone.

Jeremiah wants us to seek wisdom. He wants the saints to spend time in prayer and trust God in faith for the outcome of our lives. It may be a job-related position, marriage, finance, or family issues. When the red zone triggers the heart, may we listen to the call that Jeremiah said so tenderly. I know the plans I have for you says the Lord.

Yes, you guessed it the position that I took ended abruptly. God saw and warned me. God wants the best for our country also. He will often send out the red zones to warn his people to work together as we work through this great pandemic. His love is enduring for all.

LEARNING TO FORGIVE

Ephesians 4:32

Be kind and compassionate to one another, forgiving each other, just as in Christ God forgave you.

Unforgiveness is like a non-forgiveness bag full of rocks strapped on our back weighing down our posture leaving the shoulders stooped and bent. From time to time we may open the bag and drop a few fragments to the ground hoping to eliminate some of the weight. We tell ourselves that we will get rid of the little unforgiving fragments but the big ones we are going to keep. Does this sound familiar to you?

In my own life, I have had to work out forgiveness when life hurt more leaving me overwhelmed with grief. It may be that your workplace has skipped over a promotion that you deserved. Gossiping may be one of the issues that has brough pandemonium to your heart and soul when you knew full well that the subject of discussion was not true.

Jesus faced complexed issues of forgiveness and never murmured. He said, "Father, you forgive them for they know not what they do." His tender spirit is such an excellent guideline for the believer,

When you have a sensitive spirit, it sometimes is hard to let go of the non-forgiving bag. Small or big areas of unforgiveness, will weigh down the beautiful spirit God has given you. My prayer is that as we face the unknown challenges of war and covid that we pray with a forgiving spirit as we lead our country back to health and dignity.

LOVE POURED OUT BY A NURSE

MALACHI: 3:10

Bring the whole tithe into the storehouse, that there may be food in my house. Evaluate me in this, says the Lord.

Leadership comes from parents that are willing to take a child in their arms and lead by example. Teaching the gift of giving is a parental tool that eliminates selfishness and helps the youngster grow as he faces a world full of challenges.

As I stood in line to receive my Covid injection, the lines were unreal as Americans waited in anticipation to be inoculated. The noise of a gentlemen startled me as he yelled out to the nurse in our line to shut up talking and get on with it. The little nurse had an elderly lady that had a shirt on with a closed neck. She fumbled with the little lady's arm so she could pull out the arm without revealing her body parts. She gave the elderly lady her injection and assisted her with getting the shirt back on as to respect her modesty among a large group of people. I call this type of nursing an unselfish gift brought into the store house of America.

Tithing takes on many avenues of giving. Nurses and doctors have worked countless hours to bring hope and peace to a hurting world. The medical field in every aspect has played a part in giving. There is just something that rejuvenates the soul when we can reach out and give when life surrounds us with chaos.

My father always taught me to bring the tithe into the storehouse and you will be blessed. May we take a moment today with gratitude to thank a doctor or nurse who gives so freely. Over the years it has been so much fun to see how God is true to his word. Giving is a gift that God gave humanity.

LORD SAVE ME I AM DROWNING

Matthew 14: 22-32

St Peters personality traits were all over the place. He was impetuous, fearful, and hard to have a good relationship with.

Although he became rock solid in his faith, maturing was one of the areas on his short coming list. Jesus looked within the heart of Peter and taught him so patiently. As he matured, Jesus gave him the name of Cephas meaning Rock.

After Jesus heard of the beheading of John the Baptist, he withdrew to a place of rest. The crowds followed him and again the impetuous Peter was at the forefront. He told Jesus let us send them away. Regardless of how tired Jesus was, he asked Peter how many loaves of bread do you have? I have five then Jesus told him to bring them to him. He gave thanks and the number that was fed that day was about five thousand.

Jesus gave the disciples instructions to get in the boat and they obeyed his command. During the fourth watch of the night the storm began raging leaving the disciples fearful and afraid. Fishing in the biblical times required a lot of brawn. Peter could do the physical part of fishing but lacked faith to believe even after all the miracles that Jesus had performed in his presence. His words to Jesus, "Lord if it is you tell me to come to you on the waters," "Come he said. I can just see Peter as he climbed out of the boat, in his bravery then began to look down and call for mercy as he sank into the deep waters. Jesus reached out and lifted him saying oh you of little faith. America is facing many challenges in today's world. God cares and wants to give us the name Cephas.

GETTING RID OF CHILD LIKE BEHAVIOR

1 CORINTHIANS 13:1-13

Paul said "when I was a child, I talked like a child, I thought like a child and reasoned like a child. He goes on to tell us how important it is to put away childish behavior and look in the mirror within our souls. Whether it be in the home, workplace, or place of worship we must look for ways to be a hero.

As I walked through the store with my daughter, her big blue eyes focused on a toy that she wanted. We reasoned together as to why she should not have the toy. She looked up at me so pathetically hoping that I would sympathize with the sad look on her face. Suddenly when her methods did not work, she began to scream and fall on the floor as other adults walked by. She was a child of about 3 years old with no clue of monetary value that her desired gift cost.

In some ways children and adults are synonymous. Children will let it be known what they want openly. Adults will hide their childlike behavior through other methods. As I worked in management, I was privy to behavior that could take a department down if steps were not taken to bring stability using the team concept.

America is facing a pandemic that requires all of us to be a hero. We must go beyond the political walls for solutions that will make this great country we live in strong. The word of God gives us many examples on how to solve problems. If we take the letter I out, and work as a team putting away childish behavior all I can conceptualize is America will flourish.

THE GREAT LOVE STORY WITH JESUS

PSALM 51:10

Create in me a pure heart God and renew a steadfast spirit within me. Do not cast me from your presence or take your Holy Spirit from me. Restore to me the joy of your salvation and grant me a willing spirit, to sustain me.

Ruth had a true relationship with the God of Israel. Regardless of how much Naomi pushed her to go back to her own people she was not willing to go. Why is that? She had been in this family and learn the ways of the Israelis. She had a heart not a head relationship with the God of Israel. I love this story. Integrity is shown to all of us on what God wants from our lives. Faithfulness even when life challenges us to turn back to our old lives when life gets tough.

It must have been denigrating to Ruth to have to beg Naomi to let her stay. Pride was not in the forefront obedience to her heart and almighty God was significant. Compromise was never a choice to Ruth. God blessed her with many riches and a wonderful husband named Boaz. May we the people of God take on the attributes of Ruth when life gets tough.

Our nation has the freedom to be restored to the joy of salvation when we are willing to seek out the truth that this country was founded upon. God has a plan of opportunity for all when he said, "Come to me all that are heavy laden and I will give you peace,"

God created us to live a healthy life without margin in every part of our lives. As the Lord walks us through these touch times may we included him in our daily walk as America heals.

BALM IN GILEAD

GENESIS 37:25

Sibling rival is depicted with this chapter. Joseph's brothers despised him but was fearful as to how they were going to get rid of him. Death was not an option after all Joseph was their brother. The best choice they could produce was to sell him for twenty shekels of silver and cover it up.

In the biblical narrative, after being sold by his brother to slavery, he rose to become vizier, the second most powerful man in Egypt next to the Pharaoh. Joseph's integrity was beyond reproach. The trials that he went through with his only siblings never wavered his faith or tenacity to please God.

The ointment (Balm) was used as a healing antidote. When Joseph was put over the food during the famine in Egypt, he was a balm in Gilead. The great organizational skills that he was equipped with help feed the famine country.

When his brothers came from afar, to get food and realized their brother they sold into slavery oversaw the distribution of food, fear filled their hearts wondering what the ramification to their covered-up sin would be. The great Balm of Gilead was true forgiveness, when he told the staff to clear the room giving him the opportunity to have one on one with brothers. True forgiveness came that day for this patriarch family.

There have been times that each of us have gone through things within our life that we needed A Balm in Gilead. Lanford Wilson wrote the song depicting that we as Americans have access to the Lord Jesus Christ as our Balm in Gilead that will heal the physical as well as our emotional pain that we have faced during Covid.

CAST YOUR CARES ON HIM

Peter 5:7

Cast all your anxiety on him because he cares for you.

I stood in the early hours of the morning looking out the window hoping my husband would come home not accompanied by the police. It was about 3:00 AM. The stillness of the morning would often make me think. I was alone and the chitter chatter of the children was nestled in their beds. I ask myself what am I going to do? I only had a high school education, three little ones, and a home that was in repossession.

Alcohol and adultery destroyed my family unit. After many attempts for sobriety the 10-year marriage ended. The leadership from his precious mom and dad that served in pastoral ministry for many years, seem to fade and take the backseat to the deadly disease.

As I scrambled through the mess trying to make sense out of my life, I came to the realization that I had to go to work, I applied for a position at a nearby factory and was hired. The wages were good and the benefits impressive. The factory had an educational program for the staff who wanted to better themselves. The program was free if you kept a C average. I enrolled in classes taking one or two a quarter until I finished my degree in business.

When Peter articulated to cast all your anxieties on him, reminding us that God will walk with you during your storms of life. I caught the house payments and utilities up and the home was now in good standing. If you are out there struggling not knowing what to do during these challenging times, I am here to tell you that God took my sorrow and gave me strength to be an overcomer.

SEEKING THE GOOD FOR OTHERS

1 CORINTHIANS 10:24

Nobody should look for his own good, but the good of others. As I opened my garage door and backed out slowly, it was still dark outside. Visibility was not the best. I left earlier for work than usual on this day to give me extra time to complete a project that my place of employment asks me to do.

As I pulled into the street, I saw a little frail body walking with a cell phone in her hand. I was not sure that I knew this person, so I pulled on the main road circled around the block and drove past her again. Fearful to stop or just keep going, I caught myself putting down the window to see if everything was all right.

I looked closely into the eyes of the young woman of about 16 years of age. Five thirty in the morning was so early for a young one to be on the street. The young lady lived next door, her parents were professors and genuinely nice people. She was a teenager that was involved with other young people that was not good for her. I called her by name and said something tells me that you are up to no good. You have a cell phone in your hand and its 5:30 in the morning. She dropped her eyes at that moment. God gave me the words to say. I am going to circle the block again and I am asking you to go home. Would you do this for me I said, her little shy face nodded yes. She went home.

The parents came to my home thanking me for that moment with their daughter. I watched her over the next few years. Later I ran into her and her father in the dollar store. She let me know that she had enrolled in law school and had gotten her life together. God gives us as Christians divine moments of which we can serve others.

WORDS OF WISDOM

Psalm 19:14

Let the words of my mouth and the meditation of my heart be pleasing in your sight. This scripture is a profound tool for Christians to exemplify the word of God in their daily living. So often that is not the case. Our work world is full of people with different values and agendas to promote their own success.

The above scripture is one of my favorite scriptures. I often quote this scripture in my daily morning prayer before I start my day. I genuinely want the Lord Jesus Christ to be in the center of my life at home, work, and everyday life.

There was a situation many years ago when a staff member brought papers to me and quickly tossed them on my desk spreading the entire surface. I had to take a deep breath and call to memory Psalm 19:14. I sat there for a moment trying to wrap my mind around this type of behavior. I arose to my feet and went to her desk and ask her softly if that was the way she delivered paperwork. As I looked at her sheepish face and eyes, she said no I am sorry. Her pale face at that moment of confession, brough a ray of sunshine to her countenance.

If there is a prayer each day that I may exemplify the Lord Jesus Christ it would be Psalms 19: 14. Proverbs 21:23: He who guards his tongue keeps himself from calamity. Let us all be mindful as we start our day. When life sends challenges during the challenging times, may we step back and remember words can build or destroy.

HOPE FOR FALLEN MANKIND

Exodus 26:31-33

Make a curtain of blue, purple, and scarlet yarn and finely twisted linen.

The creation story depicts Adam and Eve as the father and mother of our nation. God created them in his image giving them access to all the trees within the garden apart from one. After the fall of humanity God still gave humanity a recourse to restore their lives. Genesis 3: 15 says "I will put enmity between you and the woman, and between your offspring and hers; he will crush your head and you will strike his heel. This is the promise of a Savior ending all the rituals and the sacrifices of the Old Testament church.

Matthew 27:51 When Jesus was born and the moment he died, the fine linen curtain that was designed for the holies of holies was torn from top to bottom. As the earth shook and the rocks split, his death was the ultimate sacrifice giving us direct access to our heavenly father for the remission of sins. He became the ultimate sacrifice with a purpose to restore man and give us a second chance.

Throughout time the bible gives so many examples of how the world seems upside down as people turned their backs leaving God out of the equation. There is hope for our nation as we look for solutions to restore and build our people. When Jesus came, the tempters power was broken. He lived and died a short life reaching out to restore his people. Let us never forget we have a Lord and Savior that wants to rebuild and restore a world in troubled times. America let the examples in the creation story and the promise of a Savior permeate our hearts today.

RUN AWAY PROPHET

JONAH 1:

The book of Jonah is one of my all-time favorites. Humanity peeks its ugly head through the runaway prophet.

JONAH 1:1

The word of the Lord came to Jonah's son of Amittai saying go to the great city of Nineveh and preach against it, because its wickedness has come up before me.

I imagine that Jonah was like most of us today. He looked at the city and saw the sin that filled the land. He looked at the people and each time in his mind he found reasons not to go there. The definition of Jonah means dove, a peaceful being, conducting and a gift from God. God saw his capabilities instructing him to go and win the loss. The challenge of ministry sent Jonah running away from the call of God. He went down to Joppa paid his fare and got aboard the ship as if to say, no God this is not for me. When we run away from God it is not the answer. Rather than look at the circumstances it is better to be obedient. The sea became his home in the belly of the fish after being thrown out of the ship by the crew member. Jonah had his special time reasoning with God and eventually giving to the call of Nineveh. When obedience filled Jonah's heart, the great fish taxi service delivered him to his place of ministry.

God has that same call for each of us. His divine purpose may be to be a teacher, a pastor, facilitator. Whatever the call may be, may we never be a runaway profit. As God brings hope to America, may we be a part in the obedience to his call as we restore our Nation.

INDIGNANT WORDS

Matthew 26:6-13

As the disciples looked at Mary of Bethany, the only thing they could see was a woman that had wasted an expensive perfume. I can just see Judas Iscariot's pious- indignant spirit as he spoke the words "Why wasn't this sold and given to the poor?"

Mary's main goal in life was to be a servant of the Lord Jesus Christ. Her sister Martha was always so busy with everyday life just like the most of us. We do not take the time to worship our Lord and Savior. The alabaster box was of immense value at least three hundred pence equivalent to a year's wages, it was Mary's best offering to the Lord. Jesus quickly rebuked Judas when he showed the insensitive remark saying that the alabaster box could have been sold to feed the poor. As I sit here writing this devotion, I can just see Mary looking up at Judas tenderly yet not wavering as she worshiped the Lord.

I once heard a young lady tell me that when people talk about Christianity that it is a sign of weakness. The bible gives us examples of true followers with great strength to we can design our life by. Mary was one of those examples. She gave her best. She was not ashamed to bow down and worship the Lord as the disciples looked judging her ack of kindness and love. This love that Mary had was true love. She never wavered regardless of the judgmental remark by Judas Iscariot. Today as you face life, and the work world may the God of Mary sink deep into your heart never wavering to the call of Worship. May we be an example in word and deeds as we serve our Risen Lord.

ANGELS ALL AROUND

Psalm 34:7

The angel of the Lord, encamps around those who fear him. As we walked the long halls of the Cleveland Clinic, my daughter asked, "Mother, which way do we go?" Together, we laughed, because Trina already knew I was directionally challenged. I loved this about her. It was how we did life together. We were a good team—always doing our best to set our fear and sorrow aside, if only for a moment, so that joy could wash over us, even during life-threatening challenges.

We entered a hospital room that was littered with medical equipment. Trina had a chemotherapy treatment scheduled for that morning. "Could you get me a cup of coffee, Mommy?" she asked me. I hurriedly left the room to see if coffee was nearby.

I noticed an older gentleman, 85 I would guess, standing by the coffee machine. As I got my coffee, he handed me another cup. "I want to make sure you don't burn your hands." His face was that of an angel. I was taken back by his kindness.

After leaving, I decided to go back and thank him for his thoughtfulness. I circled the entire floor but did not see him anywhere. And that is when I knew; God had sent an angel into my life. I smiled, grateful at God's goodness, and headed for the elevator.

When I arrived, there was a physician already in the elevator. He placed his arm around me and said, "If there is anything I can do for you, please let me know." When I stepped off the elevator, I pondered in my mind; *Who was this man—a man I did not know—who was offering help to the broken?*

I have worked many years for many doctors. But this man was different. He was willing to set all his professional rules aside to tend to my broken spirit. (God sends angels)

Trina battled stage four metastatic breast cancer. The doctors gave her three to four years to live. She lived exactly three and half years after her diagnosis. One of the things I hold so dear to my heart is how fully she lived life—never giving cancer an excuse for anger or hostility. Instead, she offered an abundance of hope and light to others. I am so proud of her.

Upon visiting President Lincoln's home, a little girl said to her mother, "Mom, Mr. Lincoln left the lights on." Well, so did my little girl. She left the lights on for all of us.

As parents, we are not programmed to lose our children. It makes no sense to us at all. We are supposed to go first. But in my experience, I have found that when this type of tragedy comes our way, God sends his angels to comfort and guide us in the most challenging times of our lives.

As we American face uncertainties in our world, God's peace and joy will bring hope to our nations as we obey him. May we leave the lights on to those that need restoration.

HUMILITY

PHILIPPIANS 2:3-4

Do nothing out of selfish ambition or vane conceit, but in humility consider others better than yourselves. Each of you should look not only to your own interest, but also to the interest of others.

The seating arrangement at the Last Supper before the crucifixion of Christ shows that Judas Iscariot selected his place at the table next to Jesus. Luke 14-8. When someone invites you to a wedding feast, do not take the place of honor, for a more distinguished than you may have been invited. Judas selected the seat right next to Jesus feeling he deserved to be the honored guest. His despicable behavior and selfishness let him to his own demise.

Sometimes in the church today we see the same behavior. People often go to the front taking the seat of honor making sure that they are recognized with importance to the house of God. Before entering the pulpit, a protracted line of adjectives is attached to the person speaking. As I write this devotion, I can just see Jesus climbing out of the boat to minister to the crowds leaving the prelude to his credentials unspoken. He simply said come unto me all ye that are heavy laden, and I will give you rest. The humility that Jesus showed on many occasions was an example that he wanted us to see. When a person is puffed up and takes their place at the table as the honored guest the downfall can be great.

My mother and father were such shy people never wanting to be up front. Cleaning, painting behind the scenes often was a job unseen and they did it so well. May we look within our hearts today for the humility of Christ as we serve others.

INTEGRITY NEVER WAVERING

Daniel 1:3-4

Then the king ordered Ashpenaz, chief of his court officials, to bring in some of the Israelites from the royal family and the nobility...young men without any physical defect handsome, showing great aptitude for learning, well informed, quick to understand and qualified to serve in the king's palace.

As I have read the history of Daniel, he was a young man of integrity and excellence. In Daniels adolescent years, his maturity was that of an elderly man. He impressed the King and was selected as one of the top leaders. I like to think his father King David and Abigail played a part in the tenacity and integrity of this young man. I believe Daniel when given a job he performed beyond the call of duty. In laypeople terms, if ask to scrub the floors, clean toilets, do yard work, he went beyond the call of duty never wavering to his social standings with the king.

The occupational status of Daniel was never a deterrent to the teaching that Daniel had received from the God of Israel. When king Nebuchadnezzar made an image of gold ninety feet high and nine feet wide. He ordered the people at the sound of the music to bow down and worship the image. Daniel would not compromise his faith for his place in the Kingdom of Nebuchadnezzar. The king threw Shadrack, Meshach and Abednego into the fiery furnace, peeking in to see their demise, discovered a fourth man that looked like the son of God. He began to praise the God of Israel. Daniel's obedience introduced the king to the God of Israel. As we face the uncertainties in the world today, may we never let the social environment, job or people denigrate our faith for the Lord Jesus Christ. America we must be strong.

DIVINE STRENGTH

Philippians 4:13

I can do all things through Christ that Strengthens me. Apostle Paul was thrown into prison for preaching the gospel. He never let that be a deterrent in ministering to the Philippians. He mentions in the scriptures of how he loved them, and he came to them with immense joy.

As Paul wrote the letter to the Church the word Joy or rejoice was used fourteen times. One might ask how he kept such a cheerful outlook. I like to call it ministering with a deep profound relationship with the God of Israel.

Paul set out to do an excellent work and the prison walls was never going to hold him back from encouraging the Saints of God. As I read this short book in the Bible, envisions of prison walls surrounding this man that never took his joy and love away. Why....... because he had a deep love for the people and wanted to carry the gospel for ages to come.

Over the years this scripture from Philippians has given me strength and courage when life seemed so hard. It has taught me to be positive when life sent me a curve ball that bounced my emotions to the ground. Paul's words played over and over in my mind. "I can do all things through Christ that strengthens me. I carried it on my being during the years that I raised my children. It was my promise from our Lord and Savior.

America we can do all things through Christ who gives us strength during the tough times.

I BELIEVE

Luke 7:6-9

Lord do not trouble yourself, for I do not deserve to have you come under my roof. That is why I did not consider myself worthy to come to you. But say the word, and my servant will be healed. I am a man of authority, with soldiers under me. I tell this one to go and he goes and that one to come and he comes. When Jesus heard this, he was amazed at him and turning to the crowd following him, he said, "I tell you, I have not found such great faith even in Israel.

A Centurion commander had many responsibilities. He would have as many as one hundred men that he oversaw. He gave out the assignments, he trained his army teaching them discipline that was harsh and brutal. One would say that the Roman army was like no other. They carried a gladius sword 18-24 inches long with a cup strapped pommel. A double edge sword designed for thrusting and stabbing because it was more deadly than being cut. The sophisticated Curriculum Vitae of the Centurion never interfered with his call as he reached out to Jesus to heal his servant.

The word of God uses servant, but I like to think that the Centurion called his servant Pai's which has ambiguous meanings associated with Child. At a moment of desperation, the Roman commander called out for mercy and healing for his child. As he approached Jesus, he called him Lord I am not worthy for you to be under my roof, say the word and my child will be healed. Accolades came from the mouth of our Lord saying I have not seen such great faith not even in Israel. If you are out there and need a miracle in your life, reach out to the Lord believing his word without your own stipulation on how God will perform the miracle. Families, children, and our great country needs a miracle today. I believe.

GOD IS THE GREAT HEALER

Matthew 15:30

Great crowds came to him, bringing the lame, the blind, the crippled, the mute and many others and laid them at his feet and he healed them.

In my devotion yesterday, I talked about the Centurion that called out to Jesus to heal his servant. His deep faith and interpersonal relationship were mentioned when he said Lord, I do not deserve you to be under my roof just say the word and my servant will be healed. I related to this story in my own life when God so miraculously healed me.

At the age of 23 years of age, I was diagnosed with Rheumatic Fever. The leakage in the vowels of my heart was of great concern to the doctor. At the time, I had one child and was instructed not to have more. Being raised in Ohio, I seldom went to church outside of my own. In June, I went to a camp meeting in Craigsville, West Virginia. The small little campground was quaint and archaic. I found it to be so inspiring and the people were so kind and loving. They had a healing service and ask that anyone who wanted God to heal them to come forward. Memory brings to my mind older ladies surrounding and putting their arms around me and praying a prayer of faith. The bleak diagnosis given by my doctor soon disappeared. As I write this devotion at the age of seventy-nine, the healing touch that my Lord gave me that night will forever encompass my soul.

My hope is today that my story along with the Centurion brings hope to someone that needs a touch from the master. Remember the Centurion said, Lord I am not worthy just say the word and I will be healed. Faith as such, can bring healing to our great country.

BLESSINGS OF HOPE

Psalm 37:9

Those who hope in the Lord will inherit the land. The meaning of hope is a feeling of trust.

As I entered the church called Peace, the land that surrounded the church was so beautifully manicured with flowers of beautiful fall colors giving you a feeling of utopia. The chairs were arranged so perfectly, and a table was set up at the back of the church with all the paraphilia to protect against Covid. The church was sparse in size; however, the people filled your hearts with their love showing kindness and acceptance to a newcomer.

During the morning service a young Asian mother came to the front of the church and announced that she and her two boys would start a Blessing Bag. They filled the bag with toothpaste, stories on God's word, can food and other items as a blessing of Hope to those less fortunate. As I sat there seeing the little ones pulling the items out of the bag, my soul rejoiced at the creativity of this mother ministering and showing her children how to minister in a crisis. The children were about four and eight. The goal was to put the bags of hope in the back of the car ready to give out when they met someone in need. As I saw the youngsters, a silhouette of hope encompassed their little faces with a glow as if to tell the world this is what life is all about.

The lesson of giving taught by the mother is one that will forever permeate the minds of the youngsters. Jesus took such a liking to children and wants we adults to have the same characteristics as we fight the battle of Covid together.

EVANGELICAL CHRISTIANS

Timothy 5:9

No widow may be put on the list of widows unless she is over sixty, has been faithful to her husband, and is well known for her virtuous deeds, such as bringing up children, showing hospitality, washing the feet of the saints, helping those in trouble and devoting herself to all kinds of honorable deeds.

The above scripture takes me back to the days when I was 19 years of age. At that time, I worked in a grocery store called Pick N Pay. Working as a cashier gave me access to many people. There were customers that you looked forward to seeing each week and would wait in line just to check out at my register.

Working in the public gives you the opportunity to minister and to be ministered to. The elderly has always been dear to my heart even as a teenager. Week after week Ms. Rosalee would come in the store and wait to check out in my line. Her stature was around five-foot-tall weighing 130 lbs. The bonnet she wore during the summer and the winter always set her apart from other customers. One day, I invited her to church and offered to pick her up in my 1953 Ford. She jumped at the chance to attend my church setting aside the differences in Evangelical and Catholicism. I learned from this dear lady how people of different faiths and political regime could come together for the good of humanity.

This is the time that we need to pull together in a team effort laying aside our differences for the great cause of our country. God is the healer not the divider.

MY SPECIAL TIME

Philippians: 4:6-7

Do not be anxious about anything, but in everything, by prayer and petition, with thanksgiving, present your request to God, which transcends all understanding will guard your heart and your mind in Christ Jesus.

At the peak of the morning hours, my little granddaughter with little blond hair and big blue eyes quietly got out of bed and came into my room and said "Nana, could I have my special time today just you and me." I got up and we made pancakes and just spent time together. This was a moment that I will never forget.

During Covid 2020, long hours within the home afforded quiet time with the Lord. When my husband left for work in the afternoon, I would go to the basement and kneel in prayer. I had a prayer chair. My prayer list consisted of family, friends, nations, churches, government, and neighbors. I felt as if God was in my garden of hope spending time with me. Covid 2020 was difficult to say the least however it brought a stillness within my soul.

From the beginning of time even after the fall of humanity, God still came to the Garden of Eden to have a conversation with the couple and giving them hope for tomorrow. He already knew that Adam and Eve sinned, yet he gave them hope for tomorrow by promising a Savior in Genesis chapter three.

As you face today, remember that God will walk with you in the challenging times as well as the enjoyable time. Like little Chloe said, I want my special time. Let us be reminded that God wants intimacy with us daily.

ALBUQUERQUE NEED

ISAIAH 58:10

And if you spend yourselves on behalf of the hungry and satisfy the needs of the oppressed then your light will rise in the darkness.

As I climbed the steps that seemed non ending to my place of employment, there was a gentlemen hovered into a fetal position leaving the earth behind hoping for a safe place to rest his frail body. He opened his eyes ever so slowly with a hint of embarrassment and said, "I am sorry." He quickly got up and headed down the stairs to find another place of shelter.

As I began my work, I could not get this young man off my mind. My thoughts rested on drugs or alcohol playing a part in his demise. I wanted to help in some way but circumstances and obligations at work became a deterrent. My thoughts during the day were filled with unspoken words and help for the needy. During the day, I prayed for this gentleman asking God to give him Hope in the mist of his brokenness.

Albuquerque is such a beautiful place sending the eyes and soul to a place of tranquility. The streets were beautiful as you walked the brick sidewalks meeting people selling homemade items to take care of their families. I wanted my light to shine and the only way I could do this for Mr. Albuquerque is to pray for him daily. God will show me the results someday.

America, let us take a moment to focus on the needs of other during moments of hopelessness. God will bring strength and hope as we serve him.

MY FRIEND BROTHER KLINE

1 JOHN 4:11

Dear friends, since God so loved us, we ought to love one another.

At the age of nineteen, I was dating a young man whose dad was the pastor of my church. He had a personality that was vibrant and never had problems articulating to strangers. As we got out of the car there was a gentleman that saw the license plates and started a conversation with me and my friend. I am not sure why he felt comfortable, but he poured out his heart saying that he had lost his children and family due to alcohol. We invited him to church that day and he surprised the both of us and came.

As the years went by, he continued to come to church never missing a service. He changed his attire and bought a suit that made him look quite handsome. Mr. Kline spoke with a lisp that distinguished him adding vibrance to his personality. When he spoke or testified in church, he glowed like a candle in the dark. The parking lot meeting was a divine appointment from God for Mr. Kline.

As the story goes, he contacted his children and reconciled the pain the children suffered during his alcoholic days. I watched this man grow in the Lord always telling how God changed his life and made him whole. These are the things that keeps me going during this great pandemic called Covid. Mr. Kline met a wonderful lady withing the church, He married, and they both worked together within the church bringing life and hope to others.

As we walked together let us not forget to love one another as Christ loved us. That is the way God is, his love is unconditional.

CARING ENOUGH TO SERVE

LUKE 10:33-34

A Samaritan, as he traveled came where the man was; and when he saw him, he took pity on him. He went to him and bandaged his wounds, pouring on oil and wine. Then he put the man on his donkey, took him to an inn and took care of him.

The scripture says that a priest was traveling the same road and saw the young man that had been beaten and robbed. He passed by on the other side as if to say it is not my parish. The Levite passed by on the other side also justifying himself with his current occupation as a helper to the priesthood. Levites often helped the priest along with other duties such as teaching and needs of the temple. I can just see the Levite moving quickly to get away from the scene of events rationalizing his own agenda for not showing mercy.

As the Samaritan passed by the young man, he had great pity and stooped down bandaged his wounds took him to the Inn and took care of him. His instructions to the Inn keeper as he handed him two silver coins "take care of him and I will give back to you for any additional expense when I return." The Samaritan cared enough to serve.

Samaritans in biblical times where shunned. The Jewish people of Galilee and Judea viewed them as a mixed race. The experts of the law would often challenge Jesus asking who is your neighbor? The Samaritan showed such mercy never thinking of his status in society. Jesus told the experts to do likewise.

Mercy is true love for humanity putting away the differences that so often divide us. Jesus gave us instructions how to serve and care for other as we serve him.

A BAG OF PENNIES

PROVERBS 16:18

Pride goes before destruction, and a haughty spirit before a fall. Better is a lowly in spirit among the oppressed than to share Plunder with the proud.

As I sat in my office, the front desk called and said they were sending back a gentleman about his account. As the young man entered my office, I gave him his account figures and ask him how he would like to pay the bill. I gave him options to select from. As he hovered over my shoulder, I could smell the night before beverage that reeked through is breath and clothing. He said, "Do you know who I am?" I quoted his name from the folder. Since I was not from the area, I was oblivious to his social standing within the area. Threats went out to my manager who instructed me to obliviate his account balance.

As I pondered the situation at hand, an older lady came in my office and introduced herself in such a cheerful way. She had a bag in her hand that was filled with pennies, nickels, quarters, and dimes. She said, I have counted this, and it is exactly what I owe. I counted it out and sure enough her account was paid in full.

Pride goes before destruction, and a haughty spirit before a fall. I learned later that the gentleman was labeled as a prominent man in the community expecting favoritism attached to his name and social standing. Jesus migrated to the lowly in spirit and oppressed society like Miss bag of pennies. Her heart was pure and honest bringing joy to the heart of God. May we find ways as Christians to bring peace when we meet people that have a haughty spirit.

MR TRACK MAN

Mark 16:15

And he said to go into all the world and preach the gospel to the whole creation.

As my husband and I pulled into the parking lot at Lowe's. My husband opened his door and quickly left the car. A gentleman with a mask on came over to the door. I lowered my window to see what he wanted. He asks if I was a Christian and as I looked deep into his eyes they were filled with tears. I quickly told him that I was and had been since I was thirteen years of age.

As he reached into his pocket, he pulled out a track telling me about the plan of salvation. The tears streaming down his red eyes touched my heart. He said, "ma'am someone led me to the Lord by simply giving me a track from the church." I go now to parking lots all over just to hand out a few tracks so that others may have the joy I have during this pandemic called Covid.

It was as if we knew each other as the dialogue continued discussing the word of God and our best friend Jesus.

As he left my presence, he said ma'am I will see you someday in heaven and we will talk again and rejoice on the streets of gold.

GOD GIVES PEACE IN THE MIST OF COVID SENDING MR TRACK MAN MY WAY TO DISCUSS OUR LORD AND SAVIOR.

RED SEA EXPERIENCE

EXODUS 14:22

The waters were divided, and the Israelites went through the sea on dry ground, with a wall of water on their right and on their left.

There are many historical events attributed to the Red Sea and the deliverance of God's people. The waters turned to blood, frogs covered the land, lice, wild animals, pestilence, boils, fiery hail, Locusts, darkness, and death of the first born. God promised Moses that he would deliver his people from the Egyptian monarchy into a land flowing with milk and honey. The current of events brough freedom to God's people. Moses being a Hebrew teacher in the 13 centuries publicized the ten commandments at Mount Sinai. It was at this point Israel became a religious community. God gave Moses a command to lead his people out of bondage and his obedience brought freedom to Israel. He is revered as one of the greatest prophets and teachers in Judaism.

There are times that we as Americans have a Red Sea experience. When the trials come, he parts the waters for us to walk through on dry land. God wants to have a deep personal relationship with us just as he did in the days of Moses. Has God asked you to do something that you are not willing to do just like Pharaoh? If so, obedience is the best alternative for peace and hope. God's people have a special bond that gives then access to the throne of grace when we pray. The word of God still stands today giving hope to a nation that so desperately needs God. Moses struggled with taking leadership of Israel. Leadership is hard but God gave him interpersonal tools to lead his people. When you are called to minister for our Lord and Savior, God will give you the tools to complete his command.

WHAT CAN WE DO FOR GOD?

Corinthians 10:3

So, whether you eat or drink or whatever you do, do it all for the glory of God.

As we live our lives for the Lord Jesus Christ, he looks within the heart to see what he can use for his glory. So often we take such pride in our work or employment but forget the people skills that bring glory to his name. Our place of employment can be used to bring hope and joy to others that may be struggling with life.

When God looks down, he is far more interested in how we stand for him than the charitable deeds we do. Deeds will go away but representation will not. How do we do that?

Many nights when I am awake, my word to the Lord is MAKE ME LIKE YOU. The fruit of the spirit is a list that God gives us in his word that will bring divine hope to a nation that is suffering.

There were times in my life, that I had to make tough choices. As I sat at my desk contemplating a certain procedure that took place within the office, I had to make a stand for what I believed in. The job was excellent with all the fringe benefits, but my soul cried out with anguish this is not biblical. I arose to my feet and resigned abruptly. There is just something special about knowing the Lord, he walks with us daily and triggers our soul with instructions.

As we serve the Lord, we can make decision of where we stand with simple word that says, THE BIBLE SAYS. As we face life today, may we always take a stand in the greatest instruction book of all time. God's word is forever true.

THE LORD LOVES A TRUTHFUL TONGUE

PROVERBS 12:22

The Lord detest lying lips, but he delights in men who are truthful.

When you are a parent, there are times that situations come to hand that requires the mom or dad to dig a little deeper to find out the truth. There was a situation in my home that I called my boys together and began to quiz them hoping to find out who was responsible. After asking each one of them if they were responsible, a quick denial. I dug a little deeper and then quickly said "If Jesus was here would you say the same thing?" As the thought pondered within their little heads all said yes except for my older son Tim. He scratched his head in deep thought respecting the deity of God and confessed.

When Jesus said that he detests a lying tongue, he knew that "when you tell a lie you must tell more lies to cover up the original lie. His words of instruction were to protect humanity.

My mom and dad brought teachings into our home that encompassed the word of God. They would often tell us to be honest in all things regardless of the outcome. In raising my own children, the concept never left me. As the police officer knocked on my door to inquire of who shot the window out of the bulldozer, my sons came to the door to answer his question. Tim gave his confession. The three hundred dollars to replace the window was nothing compared to the peace that it brough to be honest.

As we serve the Lord today, teaching our children the principle of honesty brings hope into the great Nation that we live in.

WHEN THE WINDS BLOW

Ephesian 4:14-15

Then we will no longer be infants, tossed back and forth by the waves, and blown here and there by every wind of teaching and by cunning and craftiness of men in their deceitful scheming. Instead speaking the truth in love, we will in all things grow up into him who is the Head, which is Christ.

As I stepped outside today, the sun was shining so beautifully. Every place I looked the trees were so green and a touch of fall was in the air. Nature with its golden touch has always held a special place within my heart. God created a beautiful garden of hope for humanity.

I wanted to take advantage before winter set in, so a bike ride seemed right. I put on my little red hat, sunglasses, and my mask to protect against the allergies for the season. As I began to peddle toward the south, I could go quite fast. It is easy when you are peddling away from the wind. Once I changed directions going north, the winds became strong making it exceedingly difficult to peddle.

In our Christian life we at moments have heavy winds that blow shaking our constitution wondering if we are going to make it. We face people sometimes that are crafty and deceitful that shakes the stability of our faith. We must learn to peddle against the intense winds of opposition. God promises to walk with us when we face turbulent winds as we serve him. Covid has brought turbulent winds and God will give us the tenacity to persevere.

JESUS LOVES ME THIS I KNOW

JOHN 3:16

For God so loved the world that he gave his one and only Son, that whoever believes in him shall not perish but have eternal life.

As I entered Bethany Nursing Home in Nashville, there were so many older people that just needed someone to love them. Often you would walk by, and their little hands would reach out for you hoping you would stop and spend time. There were so many that I visited that brough me so much Joy. I will share with you a gentleman that meant so much to me as a Christian.

Mr. Blind man was one that I shall never forget. His faith was Jewish. He was small of stature and his clothes swallowed him up. His hygiene did not seem to matter. The joy that permeated his face and soul seem to be infectious to those around him. As I passed him by, he reached out and said, "let me hold your hand and let us go out on the swing and sing Jesus Loves Me This I know." We walked hand in hand outside and sat on the swing his feet never touching the ground. We sang the song over and over no microphone needed. He sang with such peace and urgency knowing that the Lord that lived within him loved him.

When God created man in his image that means that God designed our genes and DNA, so Mr. Blind man sang his love song to the Lord Jesus Christ.

As we live our lives today, may we take a moment to encourage and lift those that need you to reach out with a hand of fellowship.

THE ELECTRICAL FENCE

Romans 8:6

The mind of sinful man is death, but the mind controlled by the spirit is life and peace.

One afternoon my uncle took me and my sisters to a farm that was surrounded by an electrical fence. The fence protected the animals and the beauty that nature gave to the setting. It was as if the fence was placed there as a wall of protection.

My uncle began to explain how the farmer put the fence up to keep the animals from going astray and protecting them from harm. He asks me to touch the fence evaluating the protection that it gave to the animals. He said, "go ahead and touch it you will feel a little shock." I reached out and touched the fence and quickly drew my hand back with great force. My uncle instructed me to do it repeatedly until the pain of the shock no longer caused me to remove my hand. The more I held on to the fence the easier it became. That is the way sin is. The more we commit sin the easier it gets.

God puts his arm of protection around his people as they serve him. The invisible fence designed by God gives the Saints of God protection from sinful antidotes that the world offers. The devil will often take you to a place and dialogue with you as he did in the Garden of Eden with Adam and Eve. Listen to the voice of God staying within the walls of our Lords protection.

When sin is introduced to your life, obey the internal warning that God gives to you because he loves you and wants to protect your life as you serve him.

NEVER LET YOUR DREAMS DIE

Genesis 40:15

The chief cupbearer, however, did not remember Joseph; he forgot him. We are born into this life for a purpose. The DNA within us will decide the dreams and aspirations. Our dreams are a way by which we can process emotions and goals in life.

Joseph interpreted the dreams of the cupbearer hoping that the revelation would somehow grant him a release from prison. The favor was soon forgotten, and Joseph remained in prison. I can just see the young man that was thrown in prison for deeds he did not commit, rationalizing with God as to why this had to happen. Trials of life will scratch off the rough places and make us strong. Giving up was not something that this young youth even considered. His love for God despite all the obstacles that he went through led him to become Vizier second in-command to Pharoah. Living a close life to the God of Israel attributed to the success of Joseph.

We all have dreams and goals while here in this life. We may have a dream of starting our own business, becoming a missionary so we can help the needy. Whatever God has called you to do, fill you dream with hope and love. Job was a great leader that went through many trials in life. He remained faithful to the end never allowing the denigrating remarks of failure by his friends to take away his dream. His attitude of love surfaced in Job 42-10: After Job had prayed for his friends, the Lord made him prosperous giving him twice as much as he had before. Try using the Godly wisdom of Joseph and Job. When failure came, they stepped to a new level of hope that brough peace and success.

SWEET PATRIA

Matthew 18:4

Therefore, whoever humbles himself like a little child is the greatest in the kingdom of heaven.

Teaching Sunday School gives you the opportunity to see God's grace and mercy in the lives of your students. The fourth grade is my favorite class to teach. I had a little African girl in my class that brough so much sunshine into the room. If there was a dark place, she would turn the lights on with her radiant spirit. Her little braided hair entwined with ribbons brought such beauty to her face. She brought joy to everyone she was around.

After many months of teaching Patria, I learned that her father was in prison and the stability of the home had a lot to be desired. Regardless of her surroundings, she always brought joy to those around her. The energy that she displayed made one wonder where it came from. I loved this child so much because I could see God in his fullness within her heart.

I decided to have a Valentines Party for my class. All the children were coming to my home. I received a call that Patria did not have a way to my home. I got in my car driving quickly so we would not be late. As she climbed into the car, she said, "look I bought you something." As I gazed at the little bear with a red nose, tears filled my eyes knowing the circumstances of her giving. She said, "Ms. Leda, I saved my pennies so I could buy you this special Valentine."

Happy Valentine's Day to all of you and may we have a spark within our souls that makes the heart glow like Sweet Patria.

COME BACK TO THE FATHER'S HOUSE

Luke 15:10

I tell you there is rejoicing in the presence of the angels of God over one sinner who repents.

The parable story that was used in Luke 15 illustrated a moral and spiritual lesson. The young child wanted his father to give him his inheritance early so he could make his own life. He wanted the freedom to do as he pleased. As he went out into the world to live his best life ever, he spent his money entertaining his friends living a life of corruption. The youthful eyes seemed so far away from his father's house. After spending all that he had, his eyes wandered back to his home that God had so graciously placed him in at birth.

I can just see the young man that ran away from the leadership of his father, looking back through the scrim of time remembering the good times at home and the deep love that his father had for him. When failure came, memory brought back the fact that the hired men of his father had spare food and that now he was starving. As hardship came to the prodigal, true confession came when he fell on his knees saying, "Father I have sinned against heaven and you. I am no longer worthy to be called your son."

As the prodigal son made his way back home, the father's arms opened wide accepting him with great royalty. He had a party to celebrate his return home. God has that same plan for our lives. When we leave the house of the Lord to go into the world of unknown, friends will leave us when failure comes. The heavenly father will never leave us, and his door of opportunity is always open to come home. True repentance brings rejoicing to God when we enter the portal of our heavenly home.

OTHER PEOPLE'S OPINIONS CANNOT BE MY REALITY

PSALM 9:9-10

The lord is a refuge for the oppressed, a stronghold in times of trouble. Those who know your name will trust in you, for you, Lord have never forsaken those who seek you.

In the early hours of the morning the phone rang, as I climbed out of bed, my first thoughts where it is a wrong number call. The anxiety that filled my daughter's voice soon brought great fear into my heart. She spoke softly and tenderly saying "Mother Tim has been in an accident and is in critical condition." At the time, I was living in another state and felt so helpless that I could not just get in my car and drive to him. The second phone call informed me that he had passed away. There was no pain that could compare to the losing of a child.

As I began to ponder the hurt and pain rationalizing with God telling God that Tim was studying to be in youth ministry so, please help me to understand. As time went on, I still could not rap my brain around losing my son at 23 years of age. Tim had so many great qualities that served as a witnessing tool for the Lord Jesus Christ. He reached out to the marginal youth that had problems and faced many challenging life issues.

As I entered the funeral home, my friend remarked to me that she had seen me serve God all these years and how could I ever serve him now with the losing of my child. When trouble comes, you never give up I responded. God is my refuge in the time of trouble and how could I not serve him. Life brings its challenges and his promises to never leave us it such an affirmation to our faith.

SUSTAINING GRACE

PROVERBS 3:5-6

Trust in the Lord with all your heart and lean not on your own understanding; in all your ways acknowledge him, and he will direct your path straight.

As we face the great pandemic Covid in our world, one would have to ask why is this happening? Hundreds of thousands of people have died leaving our world in such a contra. Trying to figure out where it all came from and how it came to this great country leaves Americans feeling hopeless. It is as if God put the brakes on in America and all over the world.

The good news is that we as believers have access to the throne of grace. We do not have to understand it all we just have to turn it over to the God of Israel. We are a people that often takes the matter into our own hands leaving God out of the equation. I have found in my own Christian life that I have on occasions taken matters of concern into my own hands working out a plan leaving God out.

There is a purpose when the scripture says, "Lean not on your own understanding." At times, I felt I had more insight than God. I would lay it out on paper using my knowledge at hand and continue without reservation. Every time that this occurred, I would suddenly find myself trying to dig my way out of the ditch. God sees the inevitable and his love reaches down to humanity when they acknowledge him and trust him. God's grace and mercy will bring stability to America as we lean on the Lord for wisdom and knowledge. He will give us sustaining grace.

GOD'S LITTLE ONE

Mark 10:14-15

Let the little children come to me, and do not hinder them, for the kingdom of God belongs to such as these. I tell you the truth, anyone who will not receive the kingdom of God like a little child will never enter in.

In the ancient world children were consider holding the lowest status in society. Even today, we sometimes do the same. I have heard many times the quote that children are to be seen and not heard.

I can just see the disciples as the parents began bringing their children to Jesus for a blessing, rebuke was uttered to the parents that longed for their child to be touched by the master. Value on the children was of no significance as they pushed the crowd away. I love the tender approach that Jesus took toward the little ones saying that anyone who will not receive the kingdom of God like a child will never enter in.

Teaching Sunday School gives you a great insight as to why Jesus used children as a guideline for, we adults. They are so truthful in just the simple matters. Children will often give you wisdom that you put to memory for a lifetime. Jesus saw their simplicity and their hearts and reminded we adults that we needed to take note of the characteristics and love of a child. The greatest king of all kings, (JESUS) took a liking to the little ones. May we do the same. They are the future church and foundation of this wonderful world we live in.

LOVE LIFTED ME

ROMANS 5:8

God proves his own love for us in this: While we were still sinners, Christ died for us.

Good morning to you America. There was a gentleman by the name of James Rowe that was born in England that wrote a song and published it in 1912. Rowe immigrated to the United States from Ireland in 1889. He was a Railroad worker for ten years in New York before becoming an inspector for the Hudson River Humane Society.

As I read the story attached to the dear old song "Love Lifted Me," I could not help but think that this man knew something about pain and sorrow and was looking for something that would satisfy the soul. The words I was sinking deep in sin far from the peaceful shore was words straight from his heart. The inspiration came from Matthew 14:22-23 where the disciples were in the boat and a frightening storm came, they saw Jesus' walking on the water, and he commanded Peter to come. When his faith was weak, he began to sink. Jesus lifted him up to protection. The second scripture attributed to the lyrics of the song Matthew 8:23-27 when Jesus was asleep in the boat and his disciples woke and ask for help. The arm of our Lord reached out and brought peace to the storm.

God can bring great peace to this great nation that we live in during the tough times for America. The words, I was sinking deep in sin far from the peaceful shore was a true confession that Rowe recognized hope comes to the fallen. America let us claim the peace that God gives our nation during this great pandemic.

WE CAN MAKE A DIFFERENCE

John 15:12

My commandment is this: Love each other as I have loved you.

There are times when I visit the nursing home, I ask myself if the patient really knows that I am there. When I enter the room and begin to dialogue with them silence encompassed the room as if to say I am so tired and weary. Sometimes the eyes open with such hope as you mention the words, I love you. The touch of your hand brings life into the soul of so many of the elderly.

As Ms. Margaret sat in her chair, she screamed out violently overtures of profanity requesting me to please untie her. I knelt beside her and with a soft voice told her that Jesus loves her so much. The mention of our Lord's name brought peace to the angry spirit. I visited many years with Ms. Margaret and could see the difference with just the touch of my hand and the stories of hope about our Lord and Savior.

Ms. Madeline was another dear lady that had been active in the church for many years. She had a cerebral hemorrhage that took away her speech and mobility. Often as I spoke with her, the stare in her eyes was so tender as I touched her hand. Inside this dear lady, God lived. God showed up in her countenance through her loving eyes even though she could not speak.

We can make a difference in others life when we find ways to minister. As you face this day, happiness will fill your life as you find a place to love others as Christ has loved you.

FINDING MY WAY HOME

JOHN 14:6

Jesus said to him, "I am the way, and the truth, and the life. No one comes to the father accept through me.

My mother told me the story of the day that I came into the world. At that time, she lived in Tennessee during the Pearl Harbor war. She said that the ladies within the neighborhood came to deliver me, complications came, and they delivery came feet first. She said as the lady's ran through the house trying to get me to breathe, they prayed fervently for my life.

Fast forwarding to my first memory of being challenged directionally was at the age of four-years-old. My mother moved to New Port News Virginia close to the army base. All the homes in that area looked the same. They were tall white homes with two apartments to each house. There were two bedrooms and a bath on the top floor and the living quarters had a living room and kitchen. This was my home and I still remember the dimensions and the safety of home that mother and dad supported our family.

One day I ventured across the street telling myself I will not forget how to get back home. Excitement and fear left me directionally challenged. As I walked from home to home asking each one if they knew who my mommy was, one dear lady said I will take you home honey. She held my hand and brought me to safety.

That is the way Jesus is. In the verse above he says, "I am the way and the truth and life. When you feel lost, reach out to the master, he will take your hand and lead you to safety.

LIVING WATERS

JOHN 4:14

Jesus answered, everyone who drinks this water will be thirsty again, but whoever drinks the water I give him will never thirst.

Indeed, the water I give him will become in him a spring of living water welling up to eternal life.

As the Samaritan woman approached the well knowing full well that Jews and Samaritans were not of the same spiritual background. As Jesus dialogued with the Samaritan his goal was to give her living water that would sustain her forever. It never occurred to him that she was not of his liking. She needed the living water that he so freely gave for humanity. She was a soul that was living with a man and had five husbands prior to the relationship at hand.

As Jesus spoke to the woman, she soon became aware that his spirit had to come from God. The differences that so enthroned the Jews and Samaritans seem to fade away when a soul was at stake. Jesus came to save the world and that means everyone. His birth and death bring hope and peace to a nation if we let him.

Muddy waters so often creep into humanity derogating race color and social standing. The bible gives us so many examples of how we should live pulling all humanity to the living water that Jesus so freely gave. When we decide that people are not of our liking, the waters get muddy and cannot bring healing to the soul of man. The woman at the well had an encounter and divine appointment with God bringing hope to her brokenness. May we as Christians follow the example of our Lord and Savior leaving out pious attitudes to social and race issues.

A MOUNTAIN TO CLIMB

PSALM 121:1-2

I lift my eyes to the hills from where my strength comes from. My help comes from the Lord, the maker of heaven and earth.

Nature has always been near and dear to my heart, even as a youngster, I so enjoyed the outdoors and the beautiful gardens of hope that God so graciously gave us to enjoy here on earth.

While visiting the great state of Washington my daughter introduced me to Little Mount Si. The elevation is 1576 feet taking about 2.5 hours to complete. As I climbed, the beauty of the daisies and trees of various kinds and colors filled my eyes with wonder and made me questioned God as to how he made such a beautiful world. As I approached the top, the journey up seemed to pale as I looked down on the clouds and the scenery at the top of the mountain. I savored the moment with a hot cup of coffee feeling the great mercy and peace that this moment brought to my soul.

As I descended the mountain, the picture dimmed in comparison to the gorgeous display of artwork that God gave humanity. My body began to ache with pain as we descended. As we serve the Lord, there are many times that we have mountain top experiences that bring peace and joy to our souls. Sometimes life will bring sorrow as we make our journey to the top of God's holy heavens. The scripture, I will lift my eyes to the hills from where my strength comes from is an anchor of hope to the soul. Faithfulness is all that God needs as we make our journey to the top and descend keeping peace and joy within our hearts. The beauty that God has for us is eternal bliss when he calls us home to be with him.

DO NOT MARK THEM OFF

MATTHEW 11:28-30

Come to me, all you who are weary and burdened, and I will give you rest. Take my yoke upon you and learn from me, for I am gentle and humble in heart, and you will find rest for your soul. My yoke is easy and my burden light.

My son shared a link from his church about a young lady named Haley. As she marched into church her dress and demeanor did not seem to go along with the usual church saga that we as Christians appropriate when we attend church.

As Haley continued her weekly attendance her appearance was difference than most. None the less she wanted to be in the house of the Lord. She studied her word and became active doing her best to give her all to the Lord Jesus Christ.

God expects that we as Christian, lead people to the Lord and let the holy spirit fill their life with wisdom. My place of employment gave me opportunities to invite people to church. I would always ask God to give me that one person that I could witness to that day. A lady came in and the doors of opportunity opened. The family came to church and the loving arms of the family of God welcomed this precious family.

As we serve the Lord today, may we be mindful that God has called us to plant seeds, allowing him to give growth and wisdom as the young Christian grows. When life is hard, let us take a moment to nurture as our Lord and Savior did.

JUMP IN FIRST ASK GOD FOR A BAIL OUT

PSALM 107:28

Then they cried to the Lord in their trouble, and he delivered them from their stress.

I cannot imagine America without God. The prayer has been taken out of the schools; the mention of God is no longer relevant as we instruct our children. How did this happen? Parents became busy with everyday life, and the politicians made rules to cut the foundation in which this country was founded on.

The core values of George Washington consisted of honesty, good character, and morality. One of the greatest acclamations from our first president said, "It is the duty of all nations to acknowledge the providence of Almighty God to obey his will, to be grateful for his benefits, and humbly to implore his protection." Where did this great leadership go? It makes one wonder about the apathy that America faces as we raise our children leaving the values that our forefathers brought to our Nation. George Washington tributes his success, moral values, intellectual and physical education to his mother. HOME IS A GREAT PLACE TO RESTORE.

God has blessed America may we as Christians go back to the core values that this country was founded upon. May we never be ashamed to bow our head in prayer thanking him for the wonderful blessing that he has bestowed upon us. America, let us not jump in first and ask God for a bail out. The great God that we serve in Psalm 107:28 says they cried to the Lord in their trouble, and he delivered them. As we face the uncertainties that the pandemic has brought to America, may we make a choice to go back to the core values of our forefathers.

GOD SENT THE QUAIL

NUMBERS 11:31-32

Now a wind went out from the Lord and drove quail in from the sea. It brought them down all around the camp to about three feet above the ground, as far as a day's walk in any direction.

As we look at the pandemic that America faces our hearts are saddened. Pandemonium is everywhere. People have lost their jobs and their homes, and, in many cases, they live in hotels and some in their cars. The chaotic future of our country reminds me when Israel was in the wilderness wandering looking for hope. God's desire for Israel was to lead them through their brokenness even though it was their disobedience and complaining that made the wilderness their home.

One might ask themselves what the scripture meant when it said, "Now a wind went out from the Lord and drove the quail in from the Sea." The wind to me is the Holy Spirit making provisions for the Israelis during their own pandemic.

The quail that God sent represent his mercy and grace during the most challenging time for Israel. He gave Israel hope for the future asking only for their obedience and love as he led them through the obstacles after Pharoah let them go.

America, God so loved us that he gave us his only son that we might live. Let us take this opportunity to serve and trust our Lord during the challenging times.

WHEN YOU PRAY

PSALM 5:4-6

You are not a God who takes pleasure in evil; with you the wicked cannot dwell. The arrogant cannot stand in your presence; you hate all who do wrong. You destroy those who tell lies; bloodthirsty and deceitful men the Lord abhors.

King David was a man after the heart of God. He made lots of mistakes and God called him on the sins. Acknowledgement when confronted with his sin gave him such peace and joy. When David wrote the above scripture, it was if he was addressing his own sin face to face with God stripping away his pride through admission.

After the passing of King Saul, he went on to be the King of Israel. He is still revered as a great leader never allowing his past to be his future.

As we go through these grim times America, may we take a moment to pray from the heart seeking the wisdom of almighty God as King David did. May we pray the prayer of repentance when we sin being quick to accept responsibility for deeds that has left America broken. David's prayer led him to victory and gave him a seat of honor in the presence of God.

A simple prayer that has helped me along my way is, LORD HELP ME BE JUST LIKE YOU TODAY.

JOY IN A DIVERSE CRISIS

1 Thessalonians 5:16

Be joyful always; pray continually; give thanks in all circumstances, for this is God's will for you in Christ Jesus.

As Jesus reached out to a fallen world, he came across people such as the Pharisees that became self-appointed police officers. When a woman that had lived a very sinful life learned that Jesus was dining at a Pharisees house, she gathered her Alabaster Jar of perfume equivalent to a year's wages going unannounced to the home of the Pharisee. As she stood in the presence of the Lord, she knew he was a friend of the sinners. Instructions by the Pharisees to stone her was never on the radar of our Lord. As she poured out the perfume, she stood weeping and wet his feet with tears. There was just something about Jesus that drew people to him as he left condemnation out of the equation. The desire of our Lord was to bring joy and peace to a world up-side-down.

As I looked out my back window peering at the beautiful sunshine that God gave us, a meek knock at the door took my attention away. As I opened the door, my daughter was standing there with a great big smile on her face. She said, "look mom, I brought you something." It was a joy ornament that included 1Thessalonians 5:16. I want you to be happy always mom so put this on your desk to enjoy. Her joyful personality always filled the room upon her entrance. Circumstances cannot decide our Joy, it come from deep in the soul, as we work together during this troubled time, may we leave drops of joy to humanity.

THE PAINT BUCKET

John 6:7

Philip answered Jesus and said "Eight Months wages would not buy enough bread for each one to have a bite.

As a young thirteen-year-old, when reading the word of God, I often had many doubts at the authenticity that Sunday School teachers and pastors placed on the bible stories. When Jesus spoke with Philip about the crowd of people that was coming toward him on the mountainside, he said to Philip "Where shall we buy bread for these people to eat?" Philip looking at the multitude saying Eight Months wages would not buy enough bread for each one to have a bite. Another disciple Andrew spoke up and said there is a young child with five barley loaves and five fish. Jesus took the loaves and fish and gave thanks and fed the crowd of about five thousand.

As I sat down on the ground and opened the paint bucket to complete a job given to me by my parents, I looked inside the bucket and there was about a fourth of a can of foundation paint. The story of the fish and barley loaves came to my mind with such doubt that this story had to be fabricated. As a young teenager wanting proof, I began to talk with God telling him that if these stories were true would he please prove it to me and make the paint last until the foundation was complete. As I began to paint, I soon forgot the request that I had partitioned to God and began painting as if there was a time limit to complete the job. Upon the last stroke of painting, I looked in the bucket and it was empty. God so graciously gave me affirmation that his word is forever true.

God hears the call of young teenagers that question the word of God as they mature and grow. I am thankful for the revelation that God gave me that day at thirteen that has lasted my entire life.

COME TO MY TABLE

JOHN 6:26-27

I tell you the truth, you are looking for me, not because you saw miraculous signs but because you ate the loaves and had your fill. Do not work for food that spoils, but for food that endures to eternal life.

As I entered the church one morning, my son Tim was three years old. As I explained communion to him, he said, "mom I do not want any blood and body today," My little one did not fully understand just like the disciples. Jesus called them out when he said you saw the miraculous sign, came to my table, and had your fill.

As a Christian we come to the Lord's table and select the food that looks good. We eat a bite of grace, mercy and love and leave the table satisfied. Jesus knew full well that the disciples that came to his table saw the miracles that he performed and followed him because they were famished. Jesus told the crowd not to work for food that spoils, but for food that endures forever.

As we serve the Lord, may we eat at his table with a genuine love to follow him. When trials come, may we eat from the bread of life our faithfulness, Job 13:14: After losing all his wealth, his family, and his health he spoke word of affirmation no matter how bitter the circumstances. He said, "Though you slay me, yet I will hope in you.

As you serve him today, his table is of rich food for the soul and will nourish us even when life throws a curve. America we must be strong during these troubled times.

JEALOUSY WILL DIVIDE

1 SAMUEL 18:6-8

When the men were returning home after David had killed the Philistines, the woman came out from all the towns of Israel to meet King Saul with singing and dancing, with joyful songs and tambourines and lutes, as they danced, they sang: "Saul has slain his thousands, and David his then of thousands." Saul was incredibly angry.

Saul's intense jealousy toward King David brought such division to the monarchy of Israel. Jealousy is a deep emotion that permeates the soul causing disruption to the original plan of the God of Israel.

As we look at Saul's life and his plan to kill King David the scripture brings to the forefront a seed of jealousy that in the end took him down. David worked around the sin of Saul and eventually was anointed as the King of Israel.

Interesting enough it was by Jonathan's strong intrepidity that led King David to safety regardless of Saul's desire to destroy him. Jonathan's covenant telling David to go in peace for we have sworn friendship was an example of a true and profound relationship.

As we serve God today, may we work in one accord to cross the finish line to our Heavenly home. Teamwork minus jealously will make a successful outcome. Saul's insecurities caused him to lose his kingship and be replaced by a man after God's own heart.

Sometimes we all face the desire just like Saul wanting all the recognition as we lead in the church, home, our employment, and family. God lays out a plan that will work so well if we adhere to it.

A MARK OF DISTINCTION

Genesis 6:6-8

The Lord was grieved that he had made man on the earth, and his heart was filled with pain. So, the Lord said. "I will wipe mankind, whom I have created, from the face of the earth men animals and creatures that move along the ground, and birds of the air, for I am grieved that I have made them. Noah found favor in the eyes of the Lord.

Genesis 6:8

Declares a mark of distinction for Noah when God announced that he found favor in the eyes of the Lord. His obedience and desire to serve Jehovah God earned him a special place in the heart of almighty God. When God instructed him to build an ark, he never wavered. I can just see Noah, sitting down with his family giving them the instructions that God had given him to build this large boat as a means of protection and safety. The trepidation the family must have felt to engage in this project shows that they too knew that their father had the attribute of favor as God described in Genesis 6:8. After the instructions that God gave Noah, it now became a family project.

May we as parents lead our children with standards that set them apart from the world. Family is the greatest institution next to the Church. Noah faced ridicule and mockery as he worked diligently to complete the task bringing safety to his family. May we as parents lead our families in the admonition seeking the favor of almighty God.

As we face these uncertain times in America, let us be reminded that we can build a wall of protections around our families through the tool of obedience.

I WILL NOT SLUMBER OR SLEEP

Psalm 121:3

He will not let your foot slip, he who watches over you will not slumber; indeed, he who watches over Israel will neither slumber nor sleep.

God always has a plan for our lives that we as God's people sometimes cannot fathom the increment details of his protection. Esther after learning that Haman had intentions to kill the Jews, her spirit was troubled leading her to seek help from the God of Israel. It was as if God was using the unlikely to full-fill his plan of protection. Mordecai adopted her, she was humble, she asks for nothing, and God gave her his blessing of hope for the Jews. The biblical hero saved the Jews of Persia and to this day a Jewish holiday Purim is sanctioned in memory of Esther.

As my mind goes back through the scrim of time, I can see this little Jewish girl that has lost her whole family and now God wants to use her to save his people. As she approached the king asking for his favor, her radiant spirit led the King in a direction that saved her people. Esther 6:1 gives a descriptive example of how God brought all this about. The king could not sleep and began to read the Chronicles and discovered that Haman took credit for saving the kings life when in fact it was Esther. Haman went from a place of honor to the gallows that he built for Mordecai.

In my own life as a Christian, the simplicity of which God uses to Glorify his name never ceases to amaze me. America God loves his people and depicts his love when he said I will neither slumber nor sleep.

WHAT IS TRUE COMMITMENT

2 Chronicles 16:9

For the eyes of the Lord range throughout the earth to strengthen those whose hearts are fully committed to him.

Commitment is the state or quality of being dedicated to a cause. As a young teenager of 13 years of age, I accepted the Lord as my personal Savior. As I knelt at the alter that night, I genuinely wanted God to take control of my life. The alter was full that night with leaders praying with those that came to commit their lives to the Lord. As I knelt that evening, I could feel a deep love that came from above. I genuinely wanted to be committed for the cause of Christ. I said, "Lord it is just me and you and I will serve you forever.

The world from the age of thirteen to my age of seventy-eight has changed in so many directions. The pews are filled with people that sit in a pew week after week never being fully committed. Parents at times leave their children to decide if they want to go to church instead of saying as for me and my house, we will serve the Lord. Sin has taken the church to a place of complacency not taking a stand to the biblical standards of the word of God.

Sitting in a seat of compromise leaving out the principals that this country was founded on, has brought tears to the heart of God. Jesus looked over Jerusalem and wept because of their sins. Let us make a true commitment to our Lord and Savior as we make our journey through life. Jesus reached out his hand of mercy to a world that so needed him.

HAPPINESS IS A CHOICE

JOHN 13:34-35

A new commandment I give you: Love one another as I have loved you. By this all men will know that you are my disciples.

As we start our day, may the joy that God so graciously gives us permeate our soul dropping happiness to those we meet daily. Situations and happenings cannot decide the beautiful glow that God placed within our hearts when we accepted him as our Lord and Savior.

As I entered the home of a young man of about forty sitting in a wheelchair, I sat down and begin to dialogue with him and the only things he could do was moan words out to let you know he understood what you were saying. His little face was filled with insecurities yet hope and joy peaked its way to my heart. Giving back to humanity is a happiness choice. I have found in my own life that when situations of sorrow come that I have no control of, I get up on the inside finding a way to bring joy to someone that day. I have found consolation when I take my eyes off the situation and find someone to encourage and love.

Nehemiah 8:10 Then he said to them, "Go, eat of the fat, drink of the sweet, and send portions to him who has nothing prepared for this day is holy to our Lord. Do not be grieved, for the Joy of the Lord is your strength. Jesus gave us an example when life seems tough, serving others is a recipe for inner joy. God has walked with us during Covid, and he will continue to be our shepherd through good and challenging times.

GOD CARES ABOUT THE LITTLE THINGS

Matthew 18:3

And he said, "I tell you the truth, unless you change and become like little children, you will never enter the kingdom of heaven.

Jesus saw the depth and love of children giving us instructions to change our ways and be more like a child. Teaching Sunday School over the years has made me more aware of why Jesus used children as a comparison for the way we adults pattern our lives. Children have a way of being direct, loving, forgiving and kind bundled up with a heart that is full of grace.

One morning as I began to teach, the lesson was a comparison of the attributes of our heavenly father and our biological father. As we wrapped up the lesson, a little guy with blonde hair and a personality as big as the outdoors raised his hand to speak. I called on him and he said, "Ms. Leda, those attributes that you spoke of about God are nothing like my father." I answered back by saying that Christian parents do not always give us our wants, but they give us instruction on how to be a better person just like God. I knew this family and the Godly influence they had upon their children and explained to the young man that love of a child is wrapped up in teaching them to be people of God.

Jesus on many occasions used children as a teaching tool to inform we adults to lay down the pretentious nature applying behavior that is childlike such as love, forgiveness, kindness, and grace. Children can teach us more about grace if we take the time to listen.

WHAT GIFT WILL I LEAVE FOR CHRIST

John 13:1

It was just before the Passover Feast. Jesus knew that the time had come for him to leave this world and go to the father. Having loved his own who were in the world, he now showed them the full extent of his love.

As I think of the life that Jesus lived while here on this earth, his impeccable example is a guideline for humanity to live by. He healed the sick, he reached the marginalized restoring brokenness that sin so often brings. He taught us about death and resurrection. In John chapter 11, The same Mary that poured perfume on the Lord and wiped his feet with her hair, called on him saying, "Lord the one you love is sick and died." Lazarus has been in the tomb four days. As Jesus approached the tomb, he called him out of the dark grave of death telling him to take off the grave clothes. At the close of our Lords life, he sat at the table to eat with his disciples telling them how to pattern their life after he is gone. The ultimate gift was given as he lay down his life for the sins of humanity at Calvary.

As I ponder over the life of Jesus, I must ask myself, what am I going to leave for humanity when I go home to heaven. Will I leave hope and peace in a world that is currently upside down during this great pandemic? Will I leave an example to my colleagues and family as I make my journey? Will the words of my mouth and the meditations of my heart be filled with God's Holy spirit? Mary and Martha reached out to Jesus for help about Lazarus death. Scripture says our Lord wept showing tender mercy yet bringing restoration and peace to Martha and Mary. Let him do the same for us today.

AMERICA HOLD ON TO YOUR BIRTHRIGHT

Genesis 25:29-32

Once when Jacob was cooking some stew, Esau came in from the open country, famished. He said to Jacob, "Quick, let me have some of the red stew! I am famished." Jacob replied sell me your birthright. "Look I am about to die Esau said. What good is the birthright to me? Jacob said, "Swear to me first." So, he swore and oath to him, selling out his birthright.

Our founding fathers enshrined freedom to the great country of America. We have freedoms that most countries do not have. As I look at the story of Esau and Jacob, I see a young man who was very tired and weary from life itself. Jacob caught him just at the right time and pursued the birthright that belonged to Esau. In trying to gain momentum with Jacob, Esau said, "I am famished," He let his guard down letting go of his God given birthright.

The deceptiveness used by Jacob is an example of how quickly the birthright of America can be taken away. What good is my birthright to me for I am famished explained Esau, I do not care about my rank that my father placed upon my life. I am hungry and need nourishment.

America God has given us this great country to live in, may we hold on to the principal values that this country was founded upon, let us place value on the God given birthright that he has given America. Circumstances must not replace deep commitment that we have to the core values of our Country. May God bless this great nation we live in.

AMERICA RETURNS TO GOD

1 JOHN 2:1

My dear children, I write this to you so that you will not sin. But if anybody does sin, we have one who speaks to the father in our defense.... Jesus Christ, the righteous one.

The Genesis narrative describes the trouble spirit that sin brought in the life of Jacob. I can just see Jacob rationalizing and planning a method to steal the birthright of his brother tucking away the ramification that his actions would bring to the family. Jacob was known for his cunning and deceitful ways.

Sin brought about the departure of Jacob from his family costing him 20 years when the Lord spoke to him and told him to return home. As he contemplated the return fear approached his heart remembering his sins that brought disintegration to the family unit. Failure to be obedient to his God gave him a different outlook as he approached the river and sent his family across staying a while as he wrestled with the Angel. I can just see Jacob thinking about all the things he had done and wanting to be once again part of the family. He stayed there all night and dealt with the Angel and then told the Angel to bless him. The hip socket that left him crippled is a reminder to all of us that obedience is our way of giving back to the God we serve. Grace and mercy took the forefront when Jacob and Esau met. Jacob kissed him. They were a family once again.

America God loves us so much that even when we sin and plan deceptiveness and deceit like Jacob, he will reach out his hand of mercy and bring us to the river of restoration through obedience as he did with Esau and Jacob.

THE WEDDING FEAST

MATTHEW 21:28-29

What do you think? There was a man who had two sons, He went to the first and said, "Son go and work today in the vineyard." I will not, he answered, but later changed his mind and went.

The quick dismissal by the son to take his father's instructions was very much like the Scribes and Pharisees. Scribes were a group of people whose profession was of writing and interpreting the laws of the Bible, The Pharisees were a people that was educated, political and religious leaders who influenced common people. I can just see the son when his father told him to go work in the vineyard. The authority of his father was not something that he was going to relent he was a grown man and had his own life. "I will not "yet he gave thought and obeyed his father's command. The first son said he would go to the vineyard but did not.

Jesus clearly says that the Kingdom of God will be taken away and given to people who will produce fruits. Matthew 21:43. The social status that clearly defines our Nation often gets in the way of the simple plan of salvation. The young man did a comparison of the lives of the prominent and changed his mind holding on to the principals and leadership of his father.

Jesus wants us to do that today putting on the wedding garment of righteousness and accepting his call to work in his vineyard until he calls us home to be with him. The reward that God will give us for our obedience is an invitation to the Wedding Feast of the Lamb of God.

FACING THE GIANTS IN OUR LIVES

1 Samuel 17:45

David said to the Philistine, you come against me with sword, spear, and Javelin, but I come against you in the name of the Lord God Almighty, God of the armies of Israel whom you have defiled.

The opposition that David faced as a young man in pursuit to protect Israel from the Philistines would have consumed anyone less strong. He was a young youth and the giant in his life stood nine feet tall. Gestures of laughter came from the mouth of the Philistine when he said, "Am I a dog, that you come at me with sticks." I can just see David holding the sling shot in his hand that was divinely anointed by the great God of Israel. When Eliab, David's oldest brother heard him speaking, he burned with anger at the proposition of his brother taking on the task of the Giant. Obedience by King David let the world know that there is a God in Israel.

There are times that we all have giants within our lives that we must decide as to the right thing to do. There was a time in my life that management ask me to let an employee go for no reason. The employee was phenomenal with a tender loving attitude that brought respect among her colleagues. As I walked back to my office, it was if a dark cloud encompassed me. I spent time trying to reason with upper management to no avail. I left my place of employment that day killing the giant of racism that America faces daily.

America is the land of the free and we all are brothers and sisters. King David faced the giant head on and as we work through these tumultuous times, we can do it too.

FAITH WITHOUT QUESTION

2 KINGS 4:1

The wife of a man from the company of the prophets cried out to Elisha, "Your servant my husband is dead, and you know that he revered the Lord. But now his creditor is coming to take my two boys as his slaves."

As a woman myself, I can understand the turmoil that this mother faced. As she approached Elisha for financial stability, he asks her, "Tell me what you have in your house." I have nothing there at all except for a little oil. The instructions to go to the neighbors and collect all the empty jars seemed a little ridiculous especially since she only had a little bit of oil. Faith Without Question led this dear lady to a place of hope and peace within her family. As she began to pour the oil it never stopped until the jars were all full. In her excitement she went to Elisha, and he gave her instructions to sell the oil and pay her debts.

When we are a child of the highest God, we have the same advocate with our heavenly father as the widow in 2 Kings. She totally had great faith as she went from door to door collecting the jars not knowing how they would be filled but believed that God would bring financial restoration to her family.

As I raised my own children there were times that I did not know how I was going to get them through college and give them the necessary amenities of life to be successful. I am here to tell you that the oil never ran dry. The stories of the bible are here to encourage Christian even when the instructions seem a little far out. The faith of the Widow is what God wants from his people.

GOD WILL RESTORE OUR CHILDREN

GENESIS 21:17

God heard the boy crying, and the angel of God called to Hagar from heaven and said to her, "What is the matter, Hagar? Do not be afraid; God has heard the boy crying as he lies there. Lift the boy up and take him by the hand, for I will make him into a great nation."

Sarah demanded that Abraham go to Hagar so they could have a little one in the house to execute the heritage of this great man of God. When Sarah stepped outside of God's original plan, pain came to Hagar and to Ishmael. Abraham was stressed as he put Hagar and Ishmael out in the desert. God spoke in a tender loving way telling Abraham not to be stressed about the maid servant he would make a great nation because he is your offspring.

As Hagar sat in the desert not knowing what to do, she walked away from her son because she did not want to see him die. God telling Hagar to lift the child up by the hand and I will make him a great nation was affirmation that God saw this mother that was broken and spilled out in a desert land. Genesis 21-19 says he opened her eyes and she saw a well and gave the boy a drink.

Across America, we hear of parents that have raised their families in church and somehow, they have ventured out into the desert of sin leaving the parents feeling helpless. God has a plan for our children just as he did with Hagar, He gave the child living water to sustain. We must continue to pray as Hagar leaving God to full fill his promise when we as parents raise our children in the admonition of our Lord and Savior. Hagar spoke to the Angel of God and so can we.

BREATH LIFE INTO THE DRY BONES

EZEKIEL 37:1-3

The hand of the Lord was upon me, and he brought me out by the Spirit of the Lord and set me in the middle of a valley; it was full of bones. He led me back and forth among them and I saw a great many bones on the floor of the valley, bones that were very dry. He asked me, "Son of man, can these bones live?"

In my own life God gave me opportunities to minister to others as I serve him. I worked for a company that was closing the doors after many years of being in business. They selected twelve people as peer counselors to collaborate with the dislocated workers of this company. As I worked with one young lady addicted to drugs her physical stature was beautiful. Her demeanor was truly kind and loving as if to say, please help me I am addicted. We spent time together sharing stories of hope and restoration for her life as she went through the steps to free her from her addiction.

America is facing the greatest pandemic ever. Job loss, monetary loss, business failures, churches empty and loss of life, Ezekiel was let by the spirit, "He asked, "Son of man, can these bones live again?" Ezekiel said, "O Sovereign Lord you alone know." God instructed him to breathe life into the dry bones.

God will bring healing to this great Nation that we live in as we take steps to free ourselves from the addictions that has enslaved us. As my friend walked through her addiction, she made choices to restore the brokenness within her soul. America, we know what to do to bring life into the dry bones of our Nation. May we all play a part to restore our country as we face the challenges ahead.

AMERICA'S PLUM LINE

AMOS 7:7-8

This is what he showed me: The Lord was standing by a wall that had been built true to plumb, with a plumb line in his hand. And the lord asked me, "What do you see, Amos?" "A plum line," I replied. Then the Lord said, "Look, I am setting a plumb line among my people Israel; I will spare them no longer.

As ancient architects designed buildings and structures, they needed a way to make the buildings safe and secure. The plum line was used to conduct their goals. The eyes can give you a picture of a building looking straight, but the plum line gives a more correct picture of a well-built structure.

God called Amos to inform the people of Israel of a plum line that he wanted for his people. He told Amos, "I will spare them no longer." Amos followed the Lord's command when God told him to leave his occupation as a shepherd and prophesy to my people Israel. The revelation of the basket of ripe fruit in chapter 8 saying, "The time is right for my people Israel; I will no longer spare them. The great prophet wanted to preserve Israel bringing hope and peace in the mist of pandemonium.

America, we are a nation that God can build a great structure with a plum line bringing stability and peace to our people. As we walk through the pandemic, may we find ways as Amos did to restore and rebuild the structure that this country was founded upon. We can do it together America.

JUST SAY YES

MATTHEW 5:5

Blessed are the meek for they will inherit the earth.

In yesterday's devotion I spoke of a plum line for America. One of the greatest ingredients to a successful plum line for the church is willing to accept the will of God without question.

Moses after leading Israel out of bondage he found himself right in the middle of a desert wandering for forty years attributed to the disobedience of his people. During the wandering many lessons were learned: The Ten Commandments was outlined as a basis for morality for thousands of years and embraced by two thirds of the world's population.

The meekness of this dear old man to see God's work endure through centuries of time, certainly was acquired during the tough times of the wilderness. He learned patience, kindness, and meekness. As Moses approached mount Horeb, the mountain of God, the angel of the Lord appeared to him in flames of fire from within a bush telling him to take off his shoes he was on Holy Ground. He took off his shoes and stood right in the middle of God's plan. However, Moses was prevented from entering the promise land because he struck the rock, instead of speaking to it as God instructed. Numbers 20-7-8.

The plum line is not always built instantly, as we see in the wilderness experience and the leadership of Moses. There were times that he strayed away from the divine God given instructions. As we live our lives in our great country may we seek the will of God in politics, homes, and churches throughout the nation making America strong.

WEAKNESS FADES IN THE PRESENCE OF GOD

2 SAMUEL 3:39

And today, though I am weak, and these sons of Zeruiah are too strong for me. May the Lord repay the evildoer according to his evil deeds.

Abner was the cousin of Israel's first king Saul. He was highly respected and was granted a place next to Saul at mealtime. He earned this place of honor by being a servant to the leadership of Saul. During Saul's reign the people of Israel were embroiled in war with the Philistines. Goliath taunted and challenged the power of almighty God leaving Saul feeling helpless. A young lad David accepted the challenge and brought Goliath down with a slingshot. David did not fear he knew the God of Israel.

When Joab brough Abner back to Hebron he deceptively pulled him aside and there to avenge the blood of his brother Asahel, Joab stabbed him in the stomach, and he died. 2 Samuel 3:27. David was promised kingship over Israel and Abner switched giving David control of the tribe of Benjamin. The narrative explicitly says that Joab killed Abner to avenge the blood of His brother Asahel, but one might think that another possibility was losing his rank as a general.

As we look at King David's life, even after all his success of killing the giant that taunted God's people, he had a moment of weakness when he said. "And today, though I am week, and these sons of Zeruiah are too strong for me." May the Lord repay the evildoer according to his evil deeds. America we must stay strong in the mist of the challenges that we face during the pandemic of Covid. Chaos is all around us, yet we Christians are Kings anointed by God and we will survive.

CARRYING THE TORCH OF FAITH

HEBREW 11:6

And without faith it is impossible to please God, because anyone who comes to him must believe that he exists and that he rewards those who earnestly seek him.

I love to tell of the moment that God showed up in my life when I needed him. He brought healing to me on many occasions that brought such hope and concerting memories that I shall never forget. I saw the great faith of my mom and dad that passed the torch on to the family to continue the faith.

In Luke 4:25: Paul wrote the second letter to Timothy from Rome where he was a prisoner and stood little chance of being released. He encouraged him to carry the torch of faith that had been passed down by his Grandmother Lois and his mother Eunice.

Paul instructed Timothy to preach the word in season and out of season enduring hardship carrying the torch of faithfulness. As Paul cried out to Timothy he said, "I have fought the good fight, I have finished the race, I have kept the faith. Now I have a crown of righteousness waiting for me. Paul's declaration of faith permeated the prison walls.

As America faces the challenges ahead, may we carry the torch of faith and Godly living in the family of God as Timothy did. May we pass along the faith that Paul, Lois and Eunice left this young minister of God. Let us never be ashamed to praise Gods holy name as we walk through the trials that sometimes encompass our soul. May we give hope to someone that needs a ray of sunshine just for the day and the moment. America we can do this.

A TRIBUTE TO LORETTA LYNN

PROVERBS 16:18

Pride goes before destruction and a haughty spirit before a fall. Notoriety was something that this great country star was familiar with but never sought.

As I entered the small Nazarene church in Franklin Tennessee, the morning worship had just finished. Loretta came down the aisle and sat mid-way to the front of the church. The pastor glanced back and said, Loretta, will you come and sing for us. She arose to her feet and came to the front of the church and began singing Amazing Grace, no music simple words from her heart that penetrated the soul as she captured the audience.

It was as if Loretta wanted a moment with the family of God leaving out Notoriety. She had a willingness to give of her talents when called upon. The church gave her their love respecting her privacy as she left the church that morning. I call this a God Moment.

Psalms 19-14 says, Let the words of my mouth and the meditations of my heart be acceptable unto you Lord." Loretta's desire was to leave this world and be known for her kindness to humanity. America, we can do the same as we walk through the challenging times.

INCREDIBLE FAITH

LUKE 5:26

Everyone was amazed and gave praise to God. They were filled with awe and said, "We have seen remarkable things today."

One day as Jesus was teaching the Pharisees and teachers of the law that came from Judea and Jerusalem, some men had heard of the healing of the sick and tried extremely hard to get the Paralytic in the presence of Jesus for healing. When this was not possible, they climbed on the roof and lowered him through the tiles in the middle of the crowd right in front of Jesus. Jesus saw their faith and said, "Friends your sins are forgiven."

The rulers of the law took a concerting effort to accuse Jesus of blaspheming when they said, "Who can forgive sins but God alone."

When Jesus said to the Paralyzed man, "Get up and take your mat and go home." I can just see this young man after all the years of being a paralytic raising to his feet and giving praise to God.

Healing comes in many forms. There is emotional healing, physical healing, and spiritual healing. God has the power to do all three. He proved this in Luke 5:26. As the paralytic jumped to his feet praising God, his emotional healing, physical healing, and spiritual healing was restored that day.

America needs emotional healing, physical healing, and spiritual healing. May we climb to the roof top letting ourselves down in the presence of the Lord for healing of our great nation.

GOD LOVES AMERICA

PSALM 61:1-3

Hear my cry, O God; listen to my prayer. From the ends of the earth, I call as my heart grows faint; I call to you, lead me to the rock that is higher than I. For you have been my refuge, a strong tower against the foe.

Condemnation filled Peter's life as his mind went back to his denial of Jesus during the hours prior to crucifixion. One of the high priest servant girls recognized Peter saying you were also with that Nazarene of Galilee. The second denial of Christ brought a more profuse denial tagged with an oath to consider legit. The third denial, I do not know the man" brought great distraught and condemnation to the heart and life of Peter.

In Jeremiah 17:9: The heart is deceitful above all thing and beyond cure. Although Peter in his weakest moment fearing the ramification of knowing our Lord and Savior, Jesus looked with tender compassion and could see into his heart. He knew that one day Peter would give his life for the cause of the Church and his people. Never one moment did Jesus hang on to the sin of the heart he looked at the great opportunities as Peter worked through his fears and loss of a Savior. One might ask themselves what we would have done in a situation such as Peter.

In our great country, God looks at his people with the same love as he did with Peter. The seventy-one members of the Sanhedrin were trying Jesus and fear filled Peters heart. Jesus knew his fear and looked beyond his faults. Matthew 16:18: Jesus said to Simon, "Upon this Rock, I will build my Church." When we fall America, God can raise us up and make us strong as we obey him.

STANDING FIRM

2 THESSALONIANS 13-14

But we ought always to thank God for you, brothers loved by the Lord, because from the beginning God chose you to be saved through the sanctifying work of the spirit and through belief in the truth.

Paul wrote the second letter of Thessalonians shortly after the first letter with instructions to continue the work in the church. Paul taught them that any spiritual growth would come from a personal relationship with the God of Israel. Paul wanted the church to grow in faith and be inspired by the holy spirit as he taught young Christians to stay firm in their faith when the world, they lived in was full of tribulation and unbelief.

As a teenager, a dear lady from the church brought so much love and encouragement to me. There were times that she would pass the pew and just stop to say hello and before you could say a word, she would embrace you with words of encouragement. The affect that her love brought to my life was a teaching tool as I taught Sunday School for many years. Sister Young was an angel sent here to earth to teach and show love to humanity.

Paul's writings lived within the heart and life of Sister Young, she had a deep profound love and encouraged the church to stay firm and faithful as they serve the Lord. America, we have the same opportunity to be anointed by the God of Israel. God loves us unconditionally and wants us to love him as we make our journey through life. Now is the time that we as a country take a stand for the principles that our country was founded upon as we work together during this great pandemic.

EATING AT GOD'S TABLE

PSALM 23:5

You prepare a table before me in the presence of my enemies. You anoint my head with oil, my cup overflows.

Dinner time at my home usually was around five in the evening. As the meal was being prepared, I wanted my child to have a balance meal full of nutrition that would make her healthy. Trina usually would say the blessing over the meal. This one evening her eyes look across the table inspecting each dish. She bowed her head and said, "Lord thank you for my spoon."

In our Christian walk with God, he prepares a table before us that is healthy. The food will replenish and restore us as well as those around us, Perhaps the table that God set for you is a plate of kindness for the poor widow that need someone to talk with. The second dish may include giving to the poor and needy. The third dish of Obedience is a nourishing food that we need to keep our healthy walk with God. The menu set before us includes kindness, giving, and obedience. As we finish the meal our dessert includes the anointing of our heads in the presence of our enemies. That is a table to be thankful for during these chaotic times in America.

As we look at the place setting in Psalm 23:5 we must eat a healthy diet that God has prepared for us in the presence of our enemies. Trina was a little one, and her spoon is the only thing that she could be thankful for. In adverse situations when we set at God's table, we sometimes look across the table and thank him for what we like leaving out his healthy plan for our lives. May we as Christians eat from the plate of righteousness serving God and humanity.

PRAYER CAN MOVE MOUNTAINS

MARK 9:28

But Jesus took him by the hand and lifted him to his feet, and he stood up.

As we face the uncertainty of the great Pandemic in America, the bible gives us assurance that God is still on the throne. If we looked back through the scrim of time, we see Jesus taking Peter, James and John leading them to a high mountain to teach and instruct them for his burial and resurrection. He was transfigured before them with dazzling white that pierced the eyes. As the cloud appeared and enveloped them, a voice spoke this is my son whom I love.

The affirmation that God gave the disciples that day is the same affirmation that he gives us today as we walk through the challenging times of life. Daily prayer is essential. God wants to talk with us. The example that Jesus set when he took his disciples to the mountain, teaching them to pray and leaving their mountain top experience discussion until Son of Man had risen from the dead.

As the disciples fought with their own lack of faith, Jesus once again took the little one who was mute and deaf and healed him. He took him by the hand and lifted him to his feet. God can do the same with America during these challenging times. We may take the time of quarantine and spend time in prayer for our great country.

Finding a designated prayer closet spending time with God gives you hope and emotional stability. In my own life, this is the most precious time spent. I feel his presence, his love, and his guidance as we walk through tough times in America. Let him walk with you too.

OPPOSITION CANNOT DESTROY YOUR DREAM

ROMANS 3:3-4

What is some did not have faith? Will their lack of faith nullify God's faithfulness? Not at all! Let God be true, and every man a liar. As it is written.

Although Jochebed the mother of Moses, Arron, and Miriam, was only mentioned twice in the bible, she held a high rank to motherhood. Her faith was resolute bringing a remarkable strength and trust in the promises of God. This woman had a dream for her family and in that dream, she prayed to the God of Israel exhilarating her as she made her journey.

When Pharaoh decreed that all baby boys were to be thrown into the Nile, her decision to put Moses in a basket certainly is not what we as parents would do today. She planned to protect his life regardless of the emotional price she paid as he drifted away and was caught up by Pharoah's daughter. One might say how did Jochebed endure such a loss. God put Jochebed at the forefront to lead her children setting up stability within their lives to honor the God of Israel. What a great task she took on behind the scenes to instill the faith of Israel. A lot is said in the bible about Moses, Arron, and Miriam but not so much about their mother. Behind the scenes she was powerful. Jochebed had a dream and certainly opposition could not take her dream away. As she placed Moses in the basket, her dream seemed inevitable. She had to let go and let God.

Moses was a great leader, his brother was a king, and Miriam was best known for worshiping and praising God singing as they crossed the Red Sea. What is your dream today as a mother and father of faith? Never allow opposition to dim the future of your God given dream.

WAITING UPON GOD

LUKE 1:11-13

Then an angel of the Lord appeared to him, standing at the right side of the alter of incense. When Zechariah saw him, he was startled and was gripped with fear. But the angels said to him: "Do not be afraid, Zechariah; your prayer has been heard. Your wife Elizabeth will bear you a son and you are to call him John.

As Zacharias was taking care of his priestly duties, he was praying for a son yet remembering that he was old and past the age of having children. I imagine his grief was much, as he bargained with God saying that he had seen all the commandments and regulations blamelessly in his priesthood. He wanted a child and could not understand the procrastination of Jehovah God. As he stood there pondering over his life, the angel appeared and told him not to be afraid Zacharias, your prayers have been heard. Through his excitement he asks the angel to give him a sign that these things would happen. The annoyed angel Gabriel told him that he would not speak until the child was born.

How many times have we as Christian been doubtful when praying for issues that has been consuming and has robbed us of the JOY because we want a sign ASAP? Zacharias let circumstances of advance old age decide his response to angel Gabriel requesting a sign. Disturbed by the request Gabriel said he would be speechless until the child was born.

As we face uncertainty in America may we wait with unwavering faith as God plans a divine strategy restoring America during this great pandemic. He sees the desires of our heart as he did with Zacharias so may we believe and trust without a sign.

MANEUVERING THROUGH THE QUICKSAND

JEREMIAH 1:7-8

But the Lord said to me, "Do not say, "I am only a child, you must go to everyone I send you to and say whatever I command you. Do not be afraid of them, for I am with you and will rescue you, "declares the Lord.

Jeremiah by nature was introspective and sensitive with a dash of shyness, He was chosen by God to warn Judah about its wickedness. He chose not to marry and go into full-time ministry to save Israel. God anointed Jeremiah even from the womb when he said before you were born, I set you apart. I appointed you as a prophet to the nations. At times he felt as if he was maneuvering through the quicksand when he said, "I am only a child. "Jeremiah took his eyes off the God given goal and looked at the present situation of Judah. They were burning incense to other God's and worshiping things they had made. The God of Israel was left out of the equation. God gave the prophet instructions to stand firm and do what I command you and you will overcome.

As God leads our great Nation, may we all be Jeremiah's for the Lord Jesus Christ. May we take a stand on issues that our country was founded upon. When it is popular to go with the crowd, may we disconnect and stand before God giving him the honor and praise that he so deserves.

America, we can do this when we search out the scriptures as a guideline for daily living. God will restore our nation and people as we serve him.

OVERCOMING OBSTACLES

2 Kings 7:3-4

Now there were four men with leprosy at the entrance of the city gate. They said to each other, "Why stay here until we die? If we say, "We will go into the city the famine is there, and we will die. And if we stay here, we will die. So, let us go over to the camp of the Arameans and surrender. If they spare us, we will live and if they kill us, we will die.

Sometimes God uses the inevitable to full-fill his promises to his people. As the four lepers sat at the gate weak and sick, society prohibited them from entering the city for food and shelter. Restrictions left them feeling void of hope. As God took residents within their mind, he designed a plan to save his Kingdom. The simplicity of the four Lepers that God used to save his people is a miracle. His power is not always in the grandiose things it is in the minds and heart of people who love him. The frailty of the Lepers did not deter God from using them to fulfill his plan for Israel.

As they traveled to the camp of Arameans, I can just see the expectancy on their faces. God made the provision for them in the midst of a pandemic far worse than America is facing today. He opened the doors of opportunity and wealth to his people using four Lepers to conduct the obstacles that Israel faced. Fear encroached the Arameans and they fled not wanting to be captured by Israel.

God gave us this great country and he can forever heal this land and restore our Nation to peace and stability. May we as his people be used in a straightforward way to restore America.

A FLICKER OF LIGHT

PHILIPPIANS 2:14

Do everything without complaining or arguing, so that you may become blameless and pure, children of God without fault in a crooked and depraved generation.

Enoch the father of Methuselah walked with God 300 years in a wicked generation of people that blasphemed the God of Israel. The moral depravity of his generation was so displeasing to God however the bible says he walked with God. To me that means he spent time with God giving his whole pursuit to serve God.

As we look at the generation that we live in today, one might ask if the places we go and the words we say have the essential ingredients of holiness. Enoch desired that one on one with God daily and a consciousness of his presence in his daily life. Humility is a modest or low view of one's own importance. As this prophet walked with God he diminished as God became his daily counselor. His faith was a habitual light that guided him daily. The more he walked with God the flicker of light filled his soul and spilled out on humanity.

I remember when I gave my heart to the Lord in my teenage years, a flicker of light filled my life daily, As I started my day with Bible reading and prayer it gave me strength and wisdom for the day. As an American, I want that same flickering light to always reside within my heart.

The light of the Lord Jesus Christ will bring hope and peace as America walks through the challenging times. It is often said that breakfast is the most important meal of the day it replenishes your energy and alertness. Starting your day in the presence of God is like breakfast giving you spiritual wisdom and knowledge for today's tasks.

TURBULENT WATERS

GENESIS 49:3-4

Reuben, you are my first born, my might, the first sign of my strength excelling in honor, excelling in power. Turbulent as the water, you will no longer excel.

As Jacob (Israel) brought his sons in prior to his death, he said, "Gather around so I can tell you what will happen to you in days to come." His revelation to Ruben that he was powerful and was honored by all his colleagues but turbulent as water. As I read this scripture the analogy that Israel gave turbulent meaning water can be hot, cold, or warm depending on the situation at hand. I am sure as Israel looked down deep into his son's life that he wanted the turbulent water of his life to become a solid rock of faith and hope for generations to come. The words you will no longer excel, grieved the fathers heart. No parent wants to make a prediction as such to their first born.

The older I have become; I can look back on my life and see how the world has changed. There was a time that Television introduced shows of laughter and fun for the family. Today television introduces violence, sexual depravity, and disparity filling the minds of our children and young adults. The decay of our nation to hold the values of our forefathers has diminished in our nation.

As we stand in the presence of our Heavenly Father, what kind of prediction will he offer. Will the waters be turbulent, or will we take a stand on issues of life that will build our country? Reuben had the potential but the tenacity to follow God was wrapped in success and power. God wants our all America. He wants to bless us and bring healing to our Nation. Let us do it for him.

DO NOT LET TROUBLE FRAGMENT YOUR FAITH

EPHESIAN: 5:1-2

Be imitators of God, therefore as dearly loved children and live a life of love, just as Christ loved us and gave himself up for us as a fragrant offering and sacrifice to God.

The letter written to the Church at Ephesus was during the time that Paul was imprisoned in Rome around A.D.60, It never occurred to Paul to stop serving when life sent him a curve ball. I imagine as he set in the cell thinking about the ministry God called him to do, thoughts of defeat filled his mind. Questions of why God used this method to reach the people at Ephesus had to race through his thoughts. As he wrote the letter, he never complained about the hardship of the prison walls. One of the most amazing circumstances during his imprisonment was the endearment and the respect he showed to the Gentiles. PAUL LOVED WITH A CAUSE.

As I place my feet on the floor each morning, the prayer that I say is Lord Make Me Like you today. As I grew up in the church, there were times that the fragments of the church would pierce my soul as a young Christian. I wrestled with the obstacles that brought dissension within the body of Christ that did not make sense to me. Over the years, I have learned that people are people, and we must stay focused on the goal and not the circumstances.

Self-disappeared and God appeared in Paul's ministry in the lowly place of a prison cell. God sometimes uses the unusual to restore and bring peace to our land. As we face the challenges in America today, may we be a Paul for the cause of Christ.

PALPABLE LOVE

ROMANS 12:9-10

Love must be sincere. Hate what is evil; cling to what is good. Be devoted to one another in brotherly love. Honor one another above yourselves.

As I pulled into the driveway of a good friend of mine. The flowers seem to dance with beauty. There were red ones, yellow and multiple colors of blues and purples that graced the front yard of this wonderful lady. I worked many years in an environment with Ms. Ray of sunshine that was difficult especially for the female gender. It is as if the beautiful flowers in her yard permeated her personality even in challenging times. She had a twinkle in her eyes that set her apart from other employees. She worked hard, kept a positive attitude, and brought peace to the team she worked with.

After leaving Nashville and coming back home to Ohio, I had the opportunity to attend a small group with her at church. We talked about the old days that challenged our female strength and had many laughs. If I could say anything, the palpable love that penetrated her soul magnified her ability to build a team to its full potential.

This dear lady has gone on to be with the Lord now, but her legacy lives on in the lives that she touched. This is what God wants for our country to build a Nation that is founded upon integrity and love for humanity. Today as I write this, may the beautiful flowers that graced her yard, permeate, and fill my heart reminding me to dress daily with the peace and joy as I serve him.

GOD WENT BEFORE ME

DEUTERONOMY 20:4

For the Lord, your God is the one who goes with you to fight for you against your enemies to give you victory.

When we become a Christian, we have a direct line to the God of Abraham, Isaac, and Jacob. I love the above scripture that confirms that God will fight for me and give me victory over my enemies. Looking back through the scrim of time, there was a situation that I was in a car accident. It was my fault. It saddened me that another car was involved. The gentlemen in the second car mentioned that he was going to take my home, my business and everything for which I had worked. A rumor spread through my workplace of his intentions. As I contemplated the rumor, the voice within me said, "He does not know who I serve," The outcome of the suit filed by the other gentlemen took second place as God went before me as no lawyer could.

The above may seem insignificant but to me it was an important thing knowing I had children that was about to enter college and the expenses would be astronomical. I called upon God and took refuge in the scripture that God would go before me.

When King David went before Goliath, God took the most insignificant weapon a sling shot and a stone to fight against Goliath. He led Israel to victory over the Philistines. David called and God went before him. As I write this devotional Pandemonium is raging throughout America, may we call upon our Lord to bring healing to our people and Nation, Victory awaits us.

LET'S EAT BREAD TOGETHER

PSALM 23:5-6

You prepare a table before me in the presence of my enemies. You anoint my head with oil, and my cup overflows. Surely goodness and love will follow me all the days of my life and will dwell in the house of the Lord forever.

Jesus set the table in 23rd Psalm letting us know that his hand of protection stretches to all humanity to come to his table and eat the bread of life and drink from the cup of salvation. Luke 22 peaks into the heart of Jesus, He told his disciples to go into the city and they would meet a man carrying a jar of water, he instructed them to follow him home so they could have the guest room for the last supper. Jesus knew full well that this would be the last communion he would have with his disciples on earth.

When I lived in Nashville, a lady I befriend came to church. That morning we had Communion. As she took the cup, she looked at me and said, "What is this? I was not at a place that I could tell her the significance of Communion. She took the bread and the wine. After the service, I explained to her the meaning of the bread and wine.

The disciples went to the table at the last supper but did not fully understand just as my three-year-old. As they took the bread and gave thanks, Jesus told them to eat in remembrance of me. He took the wine saying this cup is the new covenant. Time brought knowledge and wisdom to his disciples after the crucifixion of our Lord. May we as Americans come to the table that God has prepared for us, He will forever walk our country and nation to peace during challenging time. The invitation is open for you today.

WHO DO YOU SAY I AM

JOB 29:18-20

I thought, "I will die in my own house, my days as many as the grains of sand. My roots will reach to the water and the dew will lie all night on my branches. My glory will remain fresh in me, the bow ever new in my hands.

Job was a man that God loved dearly. He prospered financially and was honored by the god of Abraham, Isaac, and Jacob. The word says that he was the greatest man among all the people of the East. Job was comfortable in his own house. Aversity came to the house of Job. He lost his family, identity as a righteous man, and his riches. There were many times in the book of Job that he questioned as to why God would allow such aversity when he had served him living an impeccable life that distinguished him above all men. When his friends proclaimed that his sin brought the destruction to his family, Job never wavered in his faith to God. At one point he said in Job 13:15. "Though he slays me, yet I will serve him."

Job is a book in the bible that gives you a blueprint of how to live when aversity comes your way. During his time of hardship, he talked with God daily asking the tough questions and the purpose of his hardship. It was interesting that God wanted Job to depend on him and not his friends cunning remarks as to the whys of the situation that left him poor, broken and spilled out. God restored Job in the latter part of his life more than the first part.

Job took the stand to serve God regardless of his demise and loss. America, we can do the same as we wade through this great pandemic that Covid has brought to America. Let us do it for the cause of freedom and peace. Who do you say I am? God described Job as a servant. Let us be a servant for the Lord Jesus Christ.

YOU ATE AND HAD YOUR FILL

John 6:26

I tell you the truth, you are looking for me, not because you saw miraculous signs but because you ate and had your fill.

As Jesus spoke to his disciples, saying I tell you the truth, you are looking for me not because you saw miraculous signs but because you ate and had your fill. Jesus performed many miracles at his table showing his disciples his love and mercy to humanity. Our Lord wanted them to eat from the whole table sustaining them to continue his work after his death.

The phone rang one afternoon that opened the doors of opportunity to sit at the Lord's table. The sweet voice spoke words of fear and dismay as the conversation continued. I had planned that day to do some shopping and just fun time. As she continued to speak, her voice trembled with a whimper that pierced down deep to my soul. As the youth spoke the story was one that would break the heart of our Lord and Savior. Six hours of dialogue happened that day as we sat at the Lord table of mercy and peace.

When Jesus gathered his disciples in the room, he spoke directly to them letting them know that they had ate from the table but was selective in their choices. Our Lord wanted a commitment for his cause even when their planned day become a deterrent.

If I was honest, I really wanted to shop and have fun for the day. God had other plans and I am glad that he did. America God has great plans for all of us. As we work together, may we be observant when he calls us to his table of opportunity.

FRINGE BENEFITS

PSALM 91:15

He will call upon me, and I will answer him; I will be with him in trouble, I will deliver him and honor him.

As I entered the airport, my heart began to palpitate at the mere thought of flying. My employment required me to travel and train staff all over the country. Although I loved my work, flying certainly was an area that played havoc with my emotions.

As I sat down in my seat, I whispered a prayer asking God to give me someone that could calm me during this flight of about two hours. The isle was full, and everyone seem to pass by leaving me to wonder if the seat would be occupied. The plane began to fill with passengers and the seat next to me was still empty. A tall gentlemen straggled down the aisle and stopped at my seat, He said is this seat 21A. I nodded my head yes and he sat down. I quickly told him my fear of flying and he said ma'am I am a pilot, and I will instruct you along the way every noise that you hear. As the flight continued, he told me all about flying and the mechanics of the plane. He informed me that flying is safe and to put my fears away. I felt a deep calmness to my souls as the plane landed.

When we serve the Lord, we have many fringe benefits. When we are sick, we can call on the great healer. If we need employment, God will supply the necessary means for his people. When we ask for wisdom in situations of life that we struggle with, he will instill his knowledge within our hearts.

America faces so many challenges during this great pandemic. May we as Christians reach out for the fringe benefits that he offers freely even the ones that seem so frivolous as flying.

FORFEITING YOUR MIRACLE

2 KINGS 5:10

Elisha sent a messenger to say to him, "Go wash yourself seven times in the Jordan, and your flesh will be restored, and you will be cleansed."

Faith is an area in each of our lives that illustrates our trust and belief in the God of Abraham, Isaac, and Jacob. When we have parents that illustrates faith in God, it becomes part of our DNA. "Whatsoever you ask in prayer believe, and it will be yours." Over the years, I have had the experience of God healing physically as well as emotionally when life became difficult. He became the great healer.

Naaman was a commander of the army of king Aram, He was highly regarded, and it was through him that the Lord gave victory to Arman. He was sick with Leprosy, Elisha told him to go to the Jordan river and wash yourself seven times and you will be restored. The river was filthy and Naaman did not want to stoop to such a lowly place for healing. He wanted to do it his way and not God's way. As the servant approached him and told him that if Elisha had told him to do something great, he would have adhered to the command. Dipping in the Jordan was not appealing to Naaman, however the gentle words by the servant "Wash and be clean," led him to the river and he dipped seven times and his flesh was restored.

May we as Americans not give up our miracle of healing for this great nation. May we seek wisdom from Jehovah God during this time of pandemic.

GIVING BRINGS BLESSINGS

LUKE 19:8

Zacchaeus stood up and said to the Lord, "Look Lord! Here and now, I give half of my possessions to the poor, and if I have cheated anybody out of anything, I will pay back four times the amount."

As I entered the church one morning, I looked across the aisle and saw fresh faces that I had not seen before. The church started a homeless ministry that supplied lunch and a refuge for the broken. As the service went on, the offering plate was passed by the homeless ministry, one of the gentlemen dropped several pennies in the plate of giving. I could not help but envision a tear filling the eyes of our Lord as each penny dropped in the plate.

During Jesus' time, Zacchaeus was a man that was self-enriching. He was corrupt and traitorous to the Jewish community. He was a wealthy man with no boundaries in his search for riches. Riches did not satisfy the longing within his heart. He was searching for an inner peace that would wash away the sins of his past. As he climbed the sycamore- fig tree to get a glimpse of Jesus, the mere sight of our Lord led him to inner peace. As Jesus reached the tree, he knew that Zacchaeus was looking for restoration and healing within his heart. I can just see Jesus looking up and saying come down now my child, I want to spend time with you. True confession came when the little man of stature said, "Lord here and now I will give half of my possessions to the poor and if I have cheated anybody, I will pay back four times the amount." Jesus confirmed salvation for the tax collector at once.

Although Zacchaeus traveled the road of wealth, he returned to the origin of -his name clean and pure before God. May Americans be blessed as we give systematically during this great pandemic.

UNITY BRINGS STRENGTH TO AMERICA

PSALM 133:1

How good and pleasant is it when brothers live together in unity.

Unity in the body of Christ will bring strength and power as people work together for his cause. As Jesus brought his disciples together at the last supper, he faced circumstances persistently from the Sanhedrin and the whole priestly party as to the best way to put him to death. As Jesus spoke, he said, "One of you will betray me." I can just see the twelve disciples looking at each other saying, "Lord is it I?" I envision as the Lord glanced at each one of them his eyes filled with mercy. Unity was the main dish at the table.

The conspirators wanting to take Jesus into their possession strategically planned a method of least resistance saying, "Not on the feast day, or there will be dissension among the people, Unity is not something planned it is from the very heart of God. Jesus set the example leaving mankind hope and success in a chaotic world.

As America faces the great pandemic of Covid, we must come together in Unity, we must put away I, and make decisions as we. Jesus gave that example at the last supper when he said, let us be in one accord." Jesus selected a team of men to follow him during his ministry knowing full well that one day he would be used as a sacrifice for humanity. Our Lord did it so well and with such grace and mercy.

As Americans may we come together as a team, strategically planning a method of healing for our great nation.

THERE IS A LIGHT THAT SHINES IN THE DARK

JOHN 8:12

When Jesus spoke again to the people, he said, "I am the light of the world. Whoever follows me will never walk in darkness but will have the light of life."

As I entered the drug store, I looked down at the floor that was soiled. The floor was marked with Covid signs leading to the place for inoculations. I sat down and waited 40 minutes as the hustle of clerks seemed endless. Their movement within the small area was non-stop. I could distinguish by the white coat the person that would be injecting me. As she opened the half door, "she said, "I am so sorry for the delay ma'am and thank you for your patience."

As I left the room, I looked up to see several people sitting in the chairs with such sad eyes. One gentleman of about 40ish with a hat pulled to his eyes looked up as if to say, I am tired of all this chaos. His clothes looked as if he had just gotten out of bed and rushed to the drug store to cut the long lines that Americans have faced to get their booster injection.

As I left there, I could not help but remember the scripture where Jesus said, "I am the light of the world. Whoever follows me will never walk in darkness but will have the light of life," The great proclamation by our Lord is forever true during these trouble time.

When Ezra faced pandemonium, his statement of faith, "Let us fast and petition our God about our needs and he will answer our prayer." Fasting is a method of getting close to God during the tough times. May we use this spiritual tool as America heals. THERE IS A LIGHT THAT SHINES IN THE DARKNESS AND HIS NAME IS JESUS.

REJOICING DURING OUR SUFFERING

JOHN 5:3-4

Not only so, but we also rejoice in our suffering because we know that suffering produces perseverance, perseverance character and character hope.

Shadrach, Meshach, and Abednego were three young men in their teens that faced insurmountable pressure to bow down to the golden image that Nebuchadnezzar set up in the province of Babylon. The image of gold was ninety feet high and nine feet wide. He instructed the leadership that when they heard the horn, flute, zither, lyre, harp, pipes along with the music they were to bow down and worship the image or they would be thrown into the fiery furnace.

God uses the conjectural at times to show that even in circumstances that we do not understand that his way is best. God does not have to fill in the blanks for us. The strength and fortitude of the young chaps defined their personal relationship with Jehovah God and no fiery furnace was going to deter their divine providence with God.

As the king challenged them, they said, "O Nebuchadnezzar, we do not need to defend our self if we are thrown into the blazing furnace, our God will deliver us. The God of Israel was manifested as the three young men walked out of the flames unburned or singed. Their robes were not scorched, nor did they smell of fire, A miracle as such cannot be dissected in the human brain. Nebuchadnezzar stood to his feet and said, "Praise be to the God of Shadrach, Meshach and Abednego and then promoted them to the providence of Babylon. The king was introduced to the Jehovah God through the obedience of the young men.

America God has that same plan for us during these trouble times. We must be obedient and trust even when it does not make sense as his plan unfolds during this great pandemic.

WHEN WE RUN OUT OF OPTIONS

Mark 5:27-28

When she heard about Jesus, she came up behind him in the crowd and touched his cloak, because she thought if I touch his clothes, I will be healed."

The dear lady(unnamed) in this passage of scripture had suffered twelve years under many doctors' cares. She spent all that she had and ran out of options for a cure to stop the bleeding. I can see her maneuvering back and forth through the crowd as desperation filled her eyes and face. Opportunity, she thought is only a touch away. If I can just touch his garment, I can be healed. As she reached out her hand and touched the fringe of his garment, at once the hemorrhaging stopped.

In the book of Mark 2-1-4: When Jesus entered Capernaum and word got out that he was home, so many gathered in his presence that there was no room left. As the men carried the paralytic and saw the great crowd their only choice was to climb upon the roof cut a hole and drop the paralytic down in the presence of Jesus. When Jesus saw their faith, he said, "I tell you get up and walk."

As we face the challenges that face us in the future with Covid, may we push ourselves through the maze that seem so twisted and reach out to our Lord and Savior for healing. FAITH opens the doors of opportunity during times of pain and suffering in our country.

When we love the LORD, he will supply a method in which we can stand in his presence and make our needs known to him. Sometimes we use all our options first and then we seek the Lord. Opportunity awaits America as we call on the Lord during these troubled times.

MAUNDY FOOT WASHING

JOHN 13:3-5

Jesus knew that the Father had put all things under his power, and that he had come from God and was returning to God: so, he got up from the meal, took off his outer clothing, wrapped a towel around him and washed his disciples' feet.

I grew up in a church that practiced Maundy foot washing once a year. The Thursday before Easter the church would gather with the ladies going into one room and the gentlemen another room. The pans and towel were all set up for each person to use. As I looked through the scrim of time, I could see Jesus gather his disciples together in one accord and wash their feet drying them with a towel with mercy and tenderness. Upon the completion he hugged them one by one as love spilled out.

As I enter the beautiful little church, it was graced with such a wonderful pastor and pastors' wife. The table was set for communion. The congregation's joyous spirit somehow spilled out even before the sacraments were taken. They had a joy that only salvation could bring.

When I entered the designated room for the ladies, I set on the far end of the circle. The coordinator of the service instructed someone to start the service and to select whose feet they were going to wash. Our pastor's wife stood to her feet, knelt by my chair, and began to wash my feet. As she stood, a hug of love and mercy was placed around my body. It was as if Jesus was in the room watching his people take part and humbled themselves in the sacrament of Maundy.

America may we this special time of year, take a moment to love people and serve in humility.

HE TOUCHED THE COFFIN

LUKE 7:11-12

Soon afterward, Jesus went to a town called Nain, and his disciples and a large crowd went along with him. As he approached the town gate the pallbearers were carrying a dead person, he was the only son of his mother, and she was a widow. And a large crowd from the town was with her, When the Lord saw her, his heart went out to her and he said, "Don't Cry."

There was just something about the cry heard from the widow that stirred the heart of our Lord and Savior. It was because she had lost her husband and now her only son. Her grief was incomprehensible as she walked down that lonely road that grief brings when death takes a loved one.

The heart of Jesus was stirred as he said to the widow, "Don't Cry." Jesus stretched out his hand and touched the coffin and not the body.

Young man, "I say to you, get up." The young lad sat up and began to talk as Jesus gave him back to his mother. I can just imagine when the young lad stepped out of the coffin, his desire was to take on responsibilities in a deeper and profound way serving humanity as he shredded the box that surrounded him.

America, God has a great miracle for our country. We must let Jesus touch the coffin that often surrounds Christian that are fearful to even speak his name. As the mother cried for the loss of her son, may we as Americans, cry for the healing of our Nation.

God has great plans for this great nation that we live in. May each of us accept the healing that God has instore for his people during the Covid-Pandemic.

THE TALKING DONKEY

NUMBERS 22:28

Then the Lord opened the donkey's mouth, and said to Balaam, "What have I done to you to make you beat me three times?"

The king of Moab (Balak) sent messengers to Balaam son of Beor asking him to come to his country and put a curse on the people of Egypt saying they were too powerful for him to defeat. As the conversation continued, King Balak spoke accolades of faith and trust in Balaam when he said, "For I know that those you bless are blessed and those you curse are cursed.

The flowery words and affirmation that Balak used when he said, "I will reward you handsomely if you will come and put a curse on these people. Balaam went before God seeking his divine will for the country of Moab. As Balaam talked with God, he revealed to the King that he was not to put a curse on the people because they were blessed. A second try by King Balak was on the forefront when he sent more distinguished princes to persuade Balaam to question God's authority.

As Balaam made another attempt to get confirmation by God, to eradicate God's people, the angel of the Lord with a drawn sword was placed in the path of the donkey. Rejection to move forward led Balaam to beat the donkey. God used the inevitable when the donkey said, "What have I done to cause you to beat me.? Balaam confessed before God and fell face down asking for forgiveness.

God used Balaam and the talking donkey to save the Moabites. He can use each of us during this pandemic through our obedience to serve him and humanity.

THE WELL OF LIVING WATER

JEREMIAH 2:13

My People have committed two sins: They have forsaken me, the spring of living water, and have dug their own cisterns, broken cisterns that cannot hold water.

As I think back on my own life, my parents dug a well that was priceless. At our dinner table, we all bowed our heads and dad would pray and thank God for the provision for our family. The leadership that they both showed gave their four children a love for the Lord that has lasted a lifetime. Although times were hard during those raising years dad never hesitated to drive out of his way to pick up the friends we invited to church. Mom and Dad's leadership started at adolescent until we all left home. After we left home all four children are still in church and serving God. They dug the well deep for their children.

Jeremiah spoke to Israel when he said, "I remember the devotions of your youth how as a bride you love me and followed me through the desert. He spoke with authority about the insincere worship and failure to trust Jehovah God. Jeremiah was a faithful servant. God instructed him to lead his people with authority and he listen to the voice of God. He was often called the weeping prophet. The well of leadership was deep in his soul as he prophesied that the law would be written upon the hearts of mankind.

As we face the great pandemic, in John 4:13: Jesus said, "Everyone who drinks this water will be thirsty again, but whoever drinks the water that I give him will not thirst again." May we as Americans not dig our own Cisterns but take the living water that Jesus offers.

OUR RESURRECTED LORD

Matthew 28:5

The angel of the Lord said to the woman, "Do not be afraid for I know that you are looking for Jesus, who was crucified. He is not here; he has risen, just as he said. See the place where he lay.

I can just see Mary approaching the tomb where Jesus lay, with great anticipation. She wanted to see the Lord. When the great earthquake shook the earth as the angel appeared from heaven, the heavenly aurora that surrounded the tomb brought new life. As the angel dialogued with Mary he said, "Fear not, for I know that you seek Jesus who hath been crucified," He is not here, he is risen.

Easter is a special time of the year that births new life. In America, we celebrate with new clothes and easter bonnets as we step into our place of worship. The children expect getting an Easter basket loaded with candy and topped off with a large chocolate Easter bunny. The spring of the year brings life into the daffodils and flowers that God gave humanity to enjoy. Yes (Easter) is a time for new life.

Jesus came into this world for a time and season knowing full well that one day he would be crucified for the sins of mankind. This had to be difficult during his travels, yet he never complained, He carried the cross for you and me. My father-in-law preached a sermon titled a Cross for A Broken World. As the Lord hung on the cross with his arms stretched out, he said, "Father would you forgive them for they know not what they are doing." New life was birth upon the birth and death of Jesus Christ. He holds the key to the success of our great country as we honor him daily in our lives.

ENDURANCE BRINGS ETERNAL BLISS

ROMANS 8:18

I consider that our present sufferings are not worthy comparing with the glory that will be revealed in us. There are three areas in my own life that I had to learn over the years.

I will discuss all three

1. Forgiveness: Adultery and Alcohol is a hard one to forgive especially growing up in a home with a father that's character was impeccable. My dad's character gave me a false sense of security. There came a time in my walk with Christ, I had to let it go and forgive.
2. Loving unconditional: To love unconditional is to love regardless of the hurt that you have endured. Sometimes that takes time and lots of emotional healing. There were times that I would say I forgive and yet hold on to the emotional damage that took place for me and my children.
3. Surrendering the past: When suffering takes place in our lives, we sometimes define ourselves with the pain we have endured. If we continue to define our pain, it will become self-pity. Life sometimes brings suffering and endurance brings hope to our lives and favor with the Lord.

In 2 Corinthians 11:24: Paul said, "five times I have received from the Jews the forty lashes, three time I was beaten with a rod, once I was stoned, three times I was shipwrecked, I also spent a night and day in the open sea. I have been constantly on the move. I have gone without sleep, known hunger, I have been cold and naked. Paul's words in 2 Corinthians 12:1: "I will go on to visions and revelations from the Lord," Paul's acclamation of faith is an example of endurance. Leadership in a broken world entails suffering, and Paul did that so well. May we as American endure as we face the great pandemic that Covid brings to our nation.

DELIVERANCE AND PEACE

GENESIS 32:28

Then the man said, "Your name will no longer be Jacob, but Israel, "because you have struggled with God and with men and have overcome.

Jacob being the second oldest son, aspired to receive his father Isaac's blessing regardless of how he got it. He was willing to cheat his brother Esau from the traditional blessing that goes to the oldest son. Jacob was known as a trickster going to all length to get what he wanted. His grandfather Abraham a devout man of faith and his father Isaac set an example of faith and fortitude for him to follow. Jacob stepped outside of the teachings that led him into a world of sin and deceptions.

As Jacob came face to face with himself, the haunting sting of sin permeated within his soul. It was not until he was approximately one hundred years old before he decided to draw near to God and receive God's blessing. His journey to see his brother Esau was the first step to his redemption. It was at Penuel that he came face to face with his sin and deception that he fought with the angel for deliverance. It was at Penuel that Jacob came face to face with God. His hip was dislocated signifying his deliverance.

Stories within the Bible are true examples that God gives as a role model of faith to live by. There have been times that we all wanted to take our lives in our own hands rather than follow the example that our forefathers left for us. May we as Americans come to Penuel and fight for the good of our Nation. May we stay there until the Lord gives us a new name Israel as he did with Jacob. There is no sin too great that God cannot forgive. He wants America to call upon his name for deliverance and peace.

JESUS PICKED THE OBJECTIONABLE

JOHN 20:10-11

Then the disciples went back to their homes, Verse 11: but Mary stood outside the tomb crying. As she wept, she bent over to look inside the tomb.

Mary Magdalene came from the town of Magdala located on the western sea of Galilee. Society defined her as a woman of ill repute. Mary became a woman of embodiment and devotion to the Lord and Savior. Society viewed her in roles that certainly damaged her. Her repentance brought a pot of gold to her life and heart. Gold must be melted a 19947.52 degrees Fahrenheit to bring to a melting point. The impurities rise to the top and then are scraped off before using. Mary's repentance was synonymous to a pot of gold without the impurities.

As Jesus dialogued with her, he told her to go and tell my brothers that I am alive and returning to my father in heaven. She obeys the Lord and his instructions. I can just see her leaping and crying as she made her way to the disciples. She put her past behind her and marched to victory.

Christians throughout America are struggling during these troubled times. Sin often creeps its ugly head into the hearts of God's people. Let us as Americans fill our lives with a genuine gold spilling it out on humanity as our nation heals.

God will use the objectional for his glory and will restore our great Nation.

MY ANCHOR HOLDS

ACTS 27:23-24

Do not be afraid, Paul, you must stand trial before Caesar; and God has graciously given you all the lives of all who sail with you. So, keep up your courage men, for I have faith in God that will happen just as he told me.

In Acts 27, God instructed Paul to go to Rome to preach the gospel, Paul and Silas his partner of faith boarded the Roman ship that carried cargo, prisoners, and travelers. As the ship traveled toward Rome, Paul warned the centurion of a shipwreck, but the centurion listened to the pilot and the owner of the ship. Instructions by Paul took back seat to those in charge of the boat. When the storm became fierce, Paul's courage to speak up saying, "Men you should have taken my advice not to sail from Crete; you could have spared yourselves this damage and loss."

Affirmation was given by God when the angel came to Paul and said, "Do not be afraid. God has given you all the lives who sail with you. On the 14th night around midnight the sailors felt they were close to land and began to panic. Paul instructed the commander and the soldiers saying you must stay with the ship, or it cannot be saved. Deception peaked its ugly head when the soldiers pretended, they were going to let anchors down in the front of the ship instead they cut the ropes to the lifeboats destroying the ship. It takes courage to do what Paul did in an adverse situation. God gave him wisdom to lead the ship to safety however, the commander, soldiers and owner rejected God given instructions.

America there is an anchor that holds true and will lead our nation to prosperity and healing. Be courageous and have faith as you seek wisdom from Jehovah God for our country.

TRIALS RUBBISH COMPARED TO OUR REWARDS

PHILIPPIANS 3:8

What is more, I consider everything a loss compared to surpassing greatness of knowing Christ my Lord, for whose sake I have lost all things. I consider them rubbish, that I may gain Christ.

Apostle Paul went through much persecution after he came face to face with Jesus Christ. On the road to Damascus a light from heaven flashed around him and he was blind. When the voice said, "Saul, Saul, why do you persecute me?" Conviction fell upon the heart of Paul when he said, "Who are you, Lord?" There was just something about the tender voice of Jesus that led him to be a great man of faith for the cause of Christianity.

The conversion story that took place in Paul's life on the road to Damascus is a story showing how our sovereign God used a unique way to reach the hearts of mankind. Paul was sent at an early age to Jerusalem to study. He studied with a famous rabbi, Gamaliel. He learned to write Greek and Hebrew and was well versed in the law. After Paul's conversion he endured great hardship. The book of Acts tells how the Jews accused him of desecrating the temple because he was taking Gentiles into the Holy place. He was beat, stoned, and imprisoned. The conversion story was real within his heart. Trials became rubbish compared to the loss of things and the gain of Jesus.

America, we have lost so much during this pandemic. Thousands have lost their lives; homes are broken, and the road has been rocky to say the least. May we as Americans, do as Paul did on the road to Damascus simply saying, "Who are you, Lord? "Let it be a true story of conversion for America.

JOSHUA'S COMMITMENT

JOSHUA 24:15

But as for me and my house we will serve the Lord. Joshua's commitment was truly a deep profound relationship with the God of Israel. As he sought out wisdom from God, instructions were given to him daily as he led Israel. At harvest time, the river of Jordan was at flood stage. Joshua instructed twelve men from the tribes of Israel to cross the Jordan river. He told them that when the priest carried the Ark of The Covenant that the waters flowing downward stream would be cut off and stand in a heap. The Nation of Israel crossed safely. This was the Israelites sign that God was among them.

As Israel, committed to the call of Joshua and his leadership. a memorandum of twelve stones was carried from the Jordan river to show God's blessings upon Israel.

The leadership of Joshua's life was that of obedience. He was committed to the God of Abraham, Isaac, and Jacob. Commitment is the state of quality dedicated to a cause. His love for God's chosen people was profound. God wanted them to see his protection as they came to the Jordan and the waters heaped up until they crossed safely.

America as we face the uncertainty, may we take a moment and examine our homes deciding as Joshua did when he said, as for me and my house we will serve the Lord. Compromising is not an increment part of commitment. Committed as Americans to the cause of God will lead our Nation to healing. Let us do this today!

GOD WANTS HIS SPECIAL TIME

GENESIS 3:8

Then the man and his wife heard the Lord God as he was walking in the garden in the cool of the day.

When God entered the garden of Eden in the cool of the day, his desire was to spend special time with the man and woman that he created. As he walked through the garden, he said, "Where are you?" Adam answered, "I heard you in the garden and was afraid because I was naked. As they dialoged true confession of sin removed them from the Garden of life. Even in their sin, God made garments of skin for Adam and Eve to cover their nakedness. God did not separate himself from man but made provision to walk and talk with him daily.

The disciples ask the Lord to teach them to pray in Luke 11:1. He said to them, "When you pray say: "Our Father which art in heaven, hallowed be your name. Thy kingdom come; thy will be done in earth as it is in heaven. Give us this day our daily bread, forgive us our debts, as we forgive our debtors, lead us not into temptation but deliver us from evil for thine is the kingdom and the power and glory forever Amen.

Today America as we face life together, may we as God's people lift our nation in prayer as we heal from the pain that Covid has brought to our country and nation. May we take special time to walk in the garden with God thanking him for deliverance and healing.

SCARS ARE A SIGN OF HEALING

ISAIAH 53:5

He was pierced for our transgression, he was crushed for our iniquities; the punishment that brought us peace was upon him, and by his wounds we are healed.

When I accepted Christ as my Savior, I was four months into those troubled teens when I knelt at an alter and asked God to come into my life. In my childlike mind, I thought that everything would be perfect. At the age of seventy-nine now, there have been times the bruises of life in it self-seemed incomprehensible. The loss of children, parents and family members bruised my soul. When the scars seemed to heal, Satan sends the ultimate bruise as if it would decide our love for the Lord. Commitment never yields to giving up.

Jesus walked the road to calvary giving himself for our transgressions and our sins. He was the ultimate sacrifice for humanity. Growing up as a young man, he was aware that he was sent here for a purpose, and he was committed to fulfilling God's designed plan for humanity. Matthew 12:18-20. The prophet Isaiah spoke of a savior saying, "I will put my Spirit on him, and he will proclaim justice for the nations. A bruised reed he will not break and a smoldering wick he will not snuff out. When life sends bruises stand on the promises of God. God can use our pain to help others along their way.

ANGELAS DEFINITION OF FAITH

Philippians 4:6-7

Do not be anxious about anything, but in everything, by prayer and petition with thanksgiving percent your request to God.

As I taught Sunday School one morning, the theme up for discussion was faith. Fourth grade children are just at the age that they can touch the very heart and soul of man. As I entered the room, and prepared to teach, I ask Angela to define Faith in her world. She said faith is praying for something important in your life and believing it will be done. She paused and then said, "It is like going down a long road and cannot see the end, but when you come to the end, God answers your prayer." I cannot see it, but I believe it.

Ben Carson was a great man of faith. It is said that he performed over three hundred surgeries a year. And before each surgery, he would bow his head in prayer. He averaged almost three times the average of any neurosurgeon. He grew up in Detroit and was raised by a single mother. At the age of fourteen, Ben spoke of his violent temper, but God saw a young man that needed a healing touch. It was faith in the Lord and the love of a great mother that set this young man apart in a world that needed him so desperately. Dr. Carson had a long road that he traveled and at the end of the road untold miracles happened as he obeyed Jehovah God.

As we face life today, may we pray specifically and give God the space and time to bring healing to our nation. The road has been long, but God is not finished yet. LOOK UP AMERICA!

THE JEWISH NAPKIN

JOHN 20:6-7

Then Simon Peter, who was behind him, arrived and went into the tomb, He saw the strips of linen lying there, as well as the burial cloth that had been around Jesus' head. The cloth was folded up by itself and separated from the linen.

At a Jewish dinner table, it was custom to place a napkin at each plate. The servers knew the tradition and if the guest got up and folded his napkin and laid it beside his plate that meant he was not through yet and coming back for more, if he wadded up the napkin and left the table, he was done eating.

When Jesus was placed in the tomb and arose on the third day, he folded the burial cloth to signify that he was not done yet. His work was not finished. In Luke, 24-36-49. Jesus stood among them, "Peace be with you, "at this point they recognized him. He asks them why they were troubled and doubted his resurrection. "Look at my hands and my feet," Jesus went a little further identifying his resurrection by saying, "Do you have anything here to eat?" The disciples gave him a piece of broiled fish, and he took it and ate in their presence.

Jesus left the folded napkin at his table of mercy and peace for mankind when he lived and died for humanity, He said, "This is what is written; The Christ will suffer and rise from the dead on the third day that man might have forgiveness of sins.

When we get up from our table, may we as Americans leave our napkin folded giving mercy and peace to a broken world.

GOD CHOSE YOU TO WORK FOR HIS CAUSE

JOHN 15:16

You did not choose me, but I chose you and appointed you to go and bear fruit---fruit that will last. Then the father will give you whatever you ask in his name.

Fear of failure was something that filled my life daily. Fear stopped me from going to college after my graduation from High School. I decided in my twenties to go back to school. As I walked into the classroom that day, I sat in the mid back of the room hoping no one would notice. I told myself if I failed no one would know except me and God. I gave God a promise that I would work hard, and the rest was up to him. I kept my promise and God kept his.

Obedience is a tool that God uses to full-fill his will. On the outside of me there was fear that was disguised with a professional dress and demeanor. On the inside of me there was fear and failure. John 15:16 is a scripture of affirmation that God chose me to do his work and to prepare by going back to school.

Corey Ten Boon had three visions when God called her to minister during the Holocaust. She resisted the Nazi persecution and let her family origin and experiences direct her path. She wanted a house for the prisoner, a concentration camp where she could teach the Germans to love and the third was to be released before the New Year. Corey's life was hard and difficult, but she kept her bargain and God kept his.

Failure will peak its ugly head as we serve God, but we must wait as God's plan is full filled during the process of our journey. He chose you and me to bring hope and peace to a fallen world.

A SECOND CHANCE AT LIFE

EPHESIANS 4:32

Be kind and compassionate to one another, forgiving each other, just as in Christ God forgave you.

As Apostle Paul wrote to the church his main desire was to see the church go forward. He addresses issues of husband wife, parent-children, and believers on how to bring unity within the body of Christ. Unity is the state of being united or joined as a whole. Paul's desire was to work with the church bringing prolific ideas together in peace and harmony.

Thomas A Edison had a team of men working 24 hours to make a light bulb. As the story goes, he gave the light bulb to a young chap and told him to climb the stairs. Step by step he climbed the stair and when he reached the top, he dropped it. It took another twenty-four hours to remake the bulb. Upon completion, Edison handed the bulb to the young man who dropped it the first time. Success filled Edison's life. Why was he so successful? He persevered during his failures, he worked countless hours and knew how to build the aspirations of his team.

America, God will give us a second chance. Taking the instructions that Paul gave to the church is a road map to success. One of the greatest tools in leadership is being able to look beyond the failures of the staff and pointing them to success. We can use this in the home, the church, and our families. A term that I used to use with my children when disappointments came is "YOU ARE BETTER THAN THAT SO LET'S TRY AGAIN. Our Lord and Savior believes in second chances when we mess up. Let us do it America.

AMERICA'S JOURNEY BACK HOME

PROVERBS 4:18-19

The path of the righteous is like the first gleam of dawn, shining ever brighter till the full light of day. The acceptance of Christ in my teen years, turned the lights on within my soul. I cannot imagine doing life without the radiant presence of Jesus Christ.

God defined King David as a man after his own heart. The bible gives us examples of how we must return to the road of success when we make decisions that God is displeased with. As David walked around on the rooftop, he saw a beautiful woman bathing. The outer appearance was stunning and pleasing to the eye. His first mistake was to look and then act upon his vision by sending someone to find out the details about the lovely woman. The man said, "Isn't this Bathsheba the daughter of Elam and the wife of Uriah the Hittite?" The third step was to bring her to him, and he slept with her. His eyes, mind and actions led him down a path of unrighteousness.

Satan will introduce you to sin just like he did with King David. The deceptiveness of his sin broke the heart of God. Redemption was at the forefront for the asking. In Psalms 51: David said, "Have mercy on me, O God, according to your unfailing love; according to your great compassion blot out my transgressions and wash away all my iniquity and cleanse me from my sin.

David's journey back home included repentance, admission, and restoration. May we as Americans, make our journey back home as we look at ways to become a Nation Under God's approval.

MISSED OPPORTUNITY

REVELATION 3:11

I am coming soon. Hold on to what you have, so that no one will take your crown.

The chime on my phone had an urgency that said, a friend of mine had died from Covid. As I prepared to attend the funeral, the decision to go or not to go was constantly on my mind. My thoughts were to go and sit as far back in the funeral home and exit quickly after the funeral was over. Fear gripped my heart as Covid had spread throughout America taking the lives of our loved ones.

As a youngster, Kenny was profound and wise. He was of few words but when he spoke, people listened. When in his presence, you had the lead role as you dialogued with him. It had been around 40 years since I had seen him or spoke with him. As I sat listening to people giving him accolades, my memory went back through the scrim of time affirming his love for life, his gentle spirit, and his way of making you feel like you were the most important person in the world.

God calls us to be disciples for him and often we miss his call. This day, I greeted his family, gave my condolences, and left the funeral home. I felt a tugging in my heart to go and eat and fellowship with the family. I was so fearful of Covid, I passed on the invitation. Today as I sit here writing, oh how I wish that I had not missed the opportunity to serve when God tugged at my heart.

When the opportunity comes to serve as a Christian, may we step out in faith trusting God for the outcome. Covid has restricted so many of the ministries that we love. Hold on America and never let go of the crown that God has for us.

EVERLASTING LOVE

PHILIPPIANS 2:3-4

Do nothing out of selfish ambition or vain, but in humility consider others better than yourselves. Each of you should look not only to your own interest, but also to the interest of others.

As I look at the life of Jesus, his true love for his father God exemplars a relationship that is selfless. As he worked in a broken world, he healed the sick, he raised the dead, he brought hope to the broken and spilled out. It was never about him; it was his call to serve. The scripture states that although his nature was that of God, he made himself nothing. Throughout the ministry of Jesus, he loved unconditionally, he forgave, he restored never wanting the praise of man. His love for God was not a selfish love it was genuine and filled with mercy and hope for humanity. True love for Judas Iscariot was at the forefront at the last supper. Jesus never named him as a betrayer. He loved him unconditionally.

In life, we sometimes forget how to not be selfish. It may be that our boss has assigned a work project, and upon completion, we name ourselves leaving out the efforts of the team. Proverbs 3:27 says, "Do not withhold good from those who deserve it when it is in your power to do so. "Another aspect regarding the theology of selfishness is that when we do not get the recognition that we feel we deserve, the countenance becomes downcast taking away the joy of serving without recognition.

Competition in our homes, workplace, churches, and leadership, needs to be remote and become selfless as we serve the Lord. America, we have had so many obstacles during the pandemic called Covid. Working as a team brings hope and stability to America.

AMERICA WE ARE WEAK BUT YET STRONG

PSALM 91:4-6

He will cover you with his feathers, and under his wings you will find refuge; his faithfulness will be your shield and rampart. You will not fear the terror of night, nor the arrow that flies by day, nor the pestilence that stalks in the darkness, nor the plague that destroys at midday.

There are times that we become so weak and fearful of the future that the night hours become restless. There were times in my own life that I knelt by my bed seeking refuge from almighty God, for instructions on how to solve and bring healing to the family. When I was at the end of myself, I could feel the tender touch of the Lord bringing peace to my soul. At seventy-nine, I look back at my journey he gave me untold strength along my way. He will do that for America too.

The financial stability of America is at the forefront of the politicians and leadership. There is war and sickness at every hand. America is a country that is under the hand of almighty God. May we kneel at the foot of the cross seeking his wisdom as we walk through these times of uncertainty. As I went through my own pain many years ago, the outcome was a miracle. God gave me his strength, wisdom and leadership. I love the phrase; he will cover you with his feathers. America, he will cover us with his feathers as we call upon his wisdom during this great pandemic.

May we as a country seek the wisdom of the Lord Jesus Christ as we take on the challenges during Covid. He will cover us with a shield protecting us during our journey.

MERCY SPILLED OUT

EPHESIANS 2:4-5

But because of his great love for us, God, who is rich in mercy, made us alive with Christ even when we were dead in transgressions---it is by grace you have been saved.

The correlation of the Twenty Third Psalms is paralleled to how our Lord and Savior anoints our head with his healing oil. Nose flies were such a problem in the summer months for the sheep. If the flies deposited their eggs and were successful, they would hatch in a few days and become worm-like larvae. The good Shepherd would nurture the sheep by anointing their heads with an oil of protection.

The miracles that God performed and sanctioned with his mercy shows up when Philip said in John 6:7: Philip answered and said, "Eight months wages would not buy enough bread for each one to have a bite." The amazing miracle came through a little one who had five barley loaves and two small fish. Jesus asks them to sit down and give thanks and began distributing the food. There were twelve baskets of leftovers when the meal was complete. Jesus used the unpredictable as he anointed their heads with the Shepherds oil of mercy.

America, God has given each of us a choice to accept him into our lives or to reject him. He will forgive the fallen, the adulterer, the murderer and the liar. He used his word as an example of his mercy spilled out on humanity. Apostle Paul was a man of vast knowledge and so far from God. He came to himself and was use by almighty God to set the foundation of Christianity throughout the world. God anointed Paul with the oil of protection and love. May we as Americans let the Lord Jesus Christ anoint our head daily as we serve him.

WHEN THE WINDS BLOW

MATTHEW 14:28-29

"Lord if it's you, "Peter replied, "tell me to come to you on the water." "Come," he said. Then Peter got down out of the boat, walked on the water, and came toward Jesus. But when he saw the wind, he was afraid and beginning to sink, cried aloud. "Lord Save me!"

In family situations, we all have our stories to share with each other. We laugh and sometimes we cry as we let the world inside our hearts. The stories are momentums that will always stand still within our hearts. My mother took those moments within her life. I would often see her going for a walk and finding a place to kneel and talk with the Lord. Her love and dedication left footprints within the soul and heart of me.

Jesus sent the crowd away and dismissed himself to the mountain to be alone with God. The miracle of the loaves and fishes had taken place and after feeding five thousand, he took time to give thanks to his father. At the fourth hour of the night, he appeared to his disciples walking on the water. Peter the impetuous disciple said. "Lord if it is you, tell me to come," "Come" he said. Peter like the most of us got out of the boat and began walking toward Jesus. When the wind began blowing fiercely, he took his eyes off the Savior and began to sink. As he cried out for mercy, Jesus reached out his hand and lifted him up to safety.

War is raging in Ukraine as I write this devotion, may we as Christians reach out our hand in fellowship to Ukraine as the winds of chaos blow. May we keep our eyes on the Lord never looking down during these challenging times. God loves America and he loves Ukraine.

FOOTPRINTS IN THE SAND

JEREMIAH 29:11

For I know the plans I have for you, declares the Lord. Plans to prosper you and not to harm you, plans to give you hope and a future.

Jeremiah was a young man called to minister to Judah during great wickedness. His mentor was Josiah. The political regime he faced with politics, and the religious leader had to be intimidating to say the least. His leadership was never compromised by his youth, he was called to prosper by the God of Israel. As he went to God in prayer, he said. "Ah, Sovereign Lord." I do not know how to speak; I am only a child. The Lord said to Jeremiah, "do not say, I am only a child you must go to everyone I send you to and say whatever I command you.

The connectedness that Jeremiah had with Gods chosen people was not just rhetoric it was a divine call by almighty God. His passion was to minister at all costs. As he led God's people, he certainly identified with their problems but never wavered as he confronted them with wrongdoing. In Jeremiah's leadership a quick bandage was not something that ever entered his mind. His love for the Messiah enabled him to never sacrifice his beliefs for the sake of popularity.

Jeremiah left footprints in the sand as an example of how leaders must seek wisdom from Yahweh the god of Israel. There have been many times as a Christian that the older and wiser saints left prints within my heart giving me wise instructions that made me a better person. Proverbs 13: 10 says, Pride only breeds quarrels, but wisdom is found in those who take advice. May we as Americans leave footprints in the hearts of many as we serve almighty God.

THE FALL OF JERICHO

JOSHUA 6:2-3

Then the Lord said to Joshua, "See. I have delivered Jericho into your hands, along with its king and its fighting men. March around the city once with all the armed men. Do this for six days.

Joshua was a strong man of God that listened to the inter still small voice from Jehovah for instructions on how to get his people into the promise land. When the designated spies scouted out the land and reported back to Moses and Arron the wealth and stability of the region, murmuring, complaining, and disbelief brought Israel to a standstill. When God instructed Joshua to march around the wall of Jericho for six days and the seventh day the wall would fall. This miracle was still not enough to satisfy the grumbler and complainers. At this point the leadership Moses, Arron, Joshua, and Caleb fell prostate before God asking for mercy for Israel. Israel in their unbelief gave up their place in the promise land. All that were twenty years or more sanctioned their own demise attributed to their unbelief and complaining.

At times as Christians, we do the same thing. God gives us a miracle in our lives, and we soon forget and begin to grumble and complain when life is not exactly as we think it should be. The stillness within Joshua and Caleb speaks volumes about their relationship with God. As Israel complained, they fell prostate before God seeking a solution for Israel. Sin took away the first blessing that God intended for his people.

As America faces the great challenges ahead, may we seek wisdom from Jehovah God sitting at his feet as Caleb and Joshua. God loves a man with integrity and trust.

THE TRUE VINE BRINGS LIFE TO ALL

JOHN 15:1-2

I am the true vine, and my father is the gardener. He cuts off every branch in me that bears no fruit, while every branch that does bear fruit, he prunes so that it will be even more fruitful.

The Rose is a beautiful flower that symbolizes love, beauty, and courage. As I walked into the Sunday School room to teach, I had a vase in my hand with a single rose in the vase, The lesson at hand was John 15: 1-2: I showed the class the rose that was in full bloom with radiant red pedals that sparkled as the light glimmered through the windowpanes. As the students saw the rose, they commented on its beauty and how such a small flower could bring so much life into the room.

As we discussed John 15:1-2, I told them that we would take that beautiful ray of glimmer out of the water and leave it for one week. The next Sunday, we as a class examined the rose and found that the beauty and luster had diminished significantly. The second week upon picking up the rose, the pedals fell off and the life of the Rose diminished even more.

I love how Jesus spoke to us in story form. It is as if he gave us a simple plan that we as Christians can analyze our life by. When we pull away from the vine of the Lord Jesus Christ, little by little we die spiritually. We must stay connected and let God prune our lives that we produce fruit that is pleasing to him.

As we face life today, let the Lord Jesus Christ be the true vine feeding upon his word as we serve him.

WHEN A FATHER LOVED ENOUGH TO INSTRUCT

SAMUEL 9:3

Now the donkeys belonging to Saul's father Kish were lost, and Kish said to his son Saul, "Take one of the servants with you and go and look for the donkeys.

The bible describes Saul as the son of Kish from the lineage of Benzamides as being impressive without equal among the Israelites. He stood a head taller than all the others. As Kish gave his son orders to go look for the donkeys, he obeyed his father and took a servant out with him to look for the lost animals. His life started out with such a small task that led him into kingship. Small beginnings and obedience sanctioned him as king of Israel.

Saul's demeanor was that of humility. Even after Samuel took a flask of oil and anointed his head and kissed him saying. "Has not the Lord anointed you as leader over his inheritance. The timid young man's rejections of leadership peaked through his life. When Israel asks where is the young man God has chosen? The Lord replied, "He has hidden himself among the baggage. God chose a man that was willing to do a menial task like looking for the donkeys, to bring about healing to Israel.

As Christians, we sometimes think that our curriculum must be attached with a title of Doctor or PHD to define if we are suitable for the position. The amazing thing about God is, he looked in the heart of Saul seeing his willingness to do the small task without recognition.

As Americans, may we work together during these times of trouble to bring healing to this great country of United Sates of America.

SALT OF THE EARTH

MATTHEW 27:57-58

As evening approached, there came a rich man from Arimathea, named Joseph, who had himself become a disciple of Jesus. Going to Pilate, he asked for Jesus' body and Pilate ordered that it be given to him.

When Joseph came looking for the Savior, his demeanor was that of a man not seeking notoriety. All the miracles that Jesus performed on this earth such as healing, raising the dead, restoring the wounded, giving hope to the emotional, was not at the fore front, he wanted to be close to Jesus when the acts of heroism were no longer visible. As Joseph approached Pilate asking for the body of Christ, Pilate surrendered Jesus. I envision Joseph picking the body up and taking it to the tomb wrapping linen around his body and preparing him for resurrection. What a great honor this must have been to be selected by God to carry his body to the tomb for burial.

We hear that old cliché, "Salt of the Earth" used often in description of people that we admire. Salts functionality is known for flavoring. It adds flavor to the food we eat making it more desirable for taste. As we look at Joseph's life, we see flavor as he came looking for Jesus in the evening. He was rich financially coupled with a pure heart. He loved Jesus with an agape love.

Easter is such a wonderful time to reflect on the life and resurrection of our Lord and Savior. May we as Americans become salt adding flavor to the lives of others during the tough times. Regardless of our status in life, rich, poor, businessman, mother or father let us take a stand as God heals this great nation, we live in.

LOSS OF SLEEP

ESTHER: 6:1-2

That night the king could not sleep; so, he ordered the book of the chronicles, the record of his reign, to be brought in and read to him. It was found recorded there that Mordecai had exposed Bigthana and Teresh, two of the kings' officers who guarded the doorway, who had conspired to assassinate King Xerxes.

Esther a beautiful Jewish wife of the Persian king Ahasuerus along with her cousin Mordecai brought safety and restoration to the Jews. As the king closed his eyes for sleep, the current events of the evening scrolled through his memory. When Esther asked the Jews to pray and fast as she would be going before the king seeking safety for God's Chosen People, the restless king arose from his bed wanting the Chronicles to be read. God revealed that night that Mordecai had saved his life. God had his hand upon this young Jewish woman. History says she could have been about fourteen years old when she married the king. Maturity graced her spirit and soul as she strolled through the palace honoring her God and her husband.

This story is a lesson for all of us. How many times as a parent that we have lost sleep over our children knowing that they need safety within their lives? How many times have we lost sleep over situations that we do not have control of? When we serve the Lord, we have access to the same God that Esther had. It was no accident that the king could not sleep, it was a divine moment inspired by God that the chronicles be read exposing that Mordecai had saved the king. As Mordecai took second in command next to the king, the events that circumvented around his premotion was caused by loss of sleep. God has the same plans for we Americans when we search out his perfect will in our lives.

IF WE COULD HAVE A DO OVER

EPHESIANS 5:1-2

Be imitators of God, therefore, as dearly loved children and live a life of love, just as Christ loved us and gave himself up for us as a fragrant offering and sacrifice to God.

There have been times within my life that if I could have a do over, I would have done things differently. Those moments after the collision with self we search our hearts when the tongue lashes out at a colleague, a family member, or a church member, the inter voice of our Lord and Savior speaks volumes of wisdom when he says to be an imitator of God. This has been so difficult at times for me. I would judge myself as a peaceful person but there have been times that anger filled my soul when I used my own judgment to a situation rather than using the fragrance of God.

Apostle Peter had a moment in his life denying Christ in Matthew 26: 69-74. A little girl recognized him, and Peter adamantly denied knowing Christ. A second and third chance was given to Peter to redeem himself but self and fear got in the way. Guilt by association was not something that Peter was willing to accept. The sorrow that Peter endured after the denial of knowing Jesus brought bitter weeping of regret. His do over was when he came to a place in his life that all he wanted was to be an Apostle of Jesus. Tradition has it that when Peter was crucified that he felt unworthy to be crucified like Jesus, so he requested to be crucified upside down.

In life we all have our moments that we would like to rethink our actions and have a do over. America God has a great plan for our country, and may we always seek his will never being ashamed of the Biblical values that God left as a road map to peace and Joy.

A PARENTS DELIGHT

PROVERBS 3:1-2

My Son do not forget my teachings, but keep my commandments in your heart, for they will prolong your life many years and bring you prosperity.

Many of the Proverbs came from King Solomon. He was the son of King David the shepherd boy that took down Goliath. The many experiences of Solomon led him to leave a book of wise sayings that we as parents can instruct our children as we send them out into the world.

When children go off to college, they often come home with a head full of knowledge, yet the internal values of mom and dad is still incorporated within their lives. A parent's delight is when knowledge and wisdom fill the life of their young adult so God can use them for the betterment of society.

Solomon was such a wise man, yet he did not use wisdom in selecting a wife. I am sure that his father David used his own failure as an example with Bathsheba as a teaching tool of instruction for his son. Success comes through willingness to listen and then obey.

America, we must be wise as we lead this great country back to safety during this pandemic. We must choose values that our country was founded upon. Proverbs 12: 15: says. "The way of a fool seems right to him, but a wise man listens to advice. The bible gives us wisdom and examples of failure that took place during the time of Christ. When we fail, we get up and go in a different direction just like King David.

A COVENANT WITH OUR LORD

1 SAMUEL 18:3-4

And Johnathan made a covenant with David because he loved him as himself. Jonathan took off the robe he was wearing and gave it to David, along with his tunic, and even his sword, his bow, and his belt.

As we look at the friendship of Jonathan and David, we see two men that had a spiritual bond that was sealed by God. Jonathan protected David from his own father Saul that sought out to kill the king. His display of kindness when he took off his robe, then his tunic, and went a little further by giving David his bow and his belt. He took off his own garments of protection to protect his friend. The demonstration of friendship went far beyond what the eyes could see. When Jonathan's dad Saul looked to kill David, he went to great length to protect him and the covenant of friendship. The relationship went beyond friendship, David looked after Jonathan's children long after he died. There was an unbreakable bond and covenant between the two brothers in Christ.

When Jesus died, his covenant to humanity was to bring hope and peace to a broken world. As he lived his demonstration of friendship reached to the highest mountain and the lowest valley of humanity. He stripped himself taking off the dignity of self as he hung on the cross. Even while hanging on the cross, when the criminal acknowledged Jesus was the son of God, Jesus spoke words of kindness when he said "This day you will be with me in Paradise. Luke 23:43.

America, Jesus wants to make a covenant of friendship with you today that cannot be broken as we serve him.

A CROSS FOR A BROKEN WORLD

MATTHEW 11:28-30

Come to me, all you who are weary and burdened, and I will give you rest. Take my yoke upon you and learn from me, for I am gentle and humble in heart, and you will find rest for your souls. My yoke is easy, and my burden is light.

Ira Stanphill was a young man that was saved at the age of twelve. He entered the ministry at the age of twenty-two. He would sometimes ask the congregation to suggest titles for songs. As he reached in his pocket, the words he had written down was, There's Room at the Cross. He wrote that song and the music later that evening. The impact of this dear man lives on in the hearts of so many. A crusade was being held, and a young man walked by contemplating suicide and heard someone singing Room at the Cross. He was overtaken by the message and stopped in, and his life was forever changed. He later became an evangelist for the Lord Jesus Christ.

Over the years, I have been privy to collaborating with physicians that were Psychiatrist. It seemed like a helpless world as patients sorted through their grief and sorrow. When children were part of the equation their little face took on a countenance that would make an angel cry. Even when sorrow comes to families, there is hope in the family of God. When life seems at time hard, I find myself kneeling in his presence to find peace.

America, God is giving us the same opportunity to accept him as our personal savior. The Cross is a gift that Jesus so freely gave for those that accept him. The cross can cover a multitude of sin and bring restoration to humanity.

AMERICA STANDS WITH YOU UKRAINE

ROMANS 2:8

And then the lawless one will be revealed, whom the Lord Jesus will overthrow with the breath of his mouth and destroy by the splendor of his coming.

As Ukraine faces the uncertainty of war and demise within their country, we as American stand with them. The estimated losses are at least 15K, non-fatal injuries at 1.9K. The homes and families that have been displaced is approximately 3.2 million. In February and March of 2014, Russia invaded and later annexed the Crimean Peninsula from Ukraine. This event was part of the aftermath of the Revolution of Dignity.

Greed and power are ingredient that will strip the offender of all moral values that God intended for his people. One might ask why so much pandemonium is displayed in this wonderful world that God created for man. Sin has a way of hardening the heart taking away the remorse and emotions that war brings. God's intention was that we all live in one accord.

The team concept as we face the dilemma of war is certainly a method that works. Americans have stepped up to the task as we stand together for Ukraine. May we during these times remember that the lawless will be revealed. Thank you, America, for standing alongside Ukraine.

WISDOM PREVENTS TRAGEDY

PROVERBS 4:6-8

Do not forsake wisdom, and she will protect you; love her, and she will watch over you. Wisdom is supreme; therefore, get wisdom. Though it cost all you have, get understanding. Esteem her, and she will exalt you; embrace her, and she will honor you.

George Washington was the first president of United States from 1789-1797. As he prepared to step into a role of leadership, he said he felt as if he was being led to his own execution. He felts as if he did not have the political skills to lead. He took such immense pride in his earthly name and did not want to risk it by assuming the presidency. As George Washington stepped into the role of leadership, his words of wisdom said, "I can only promise integrity and firmness as I lead."

When George Washington was fourteen, he wrote out 110 Rules of Civility in his schoolbook. My favorite rule is when he said, 'Every action done in the company, ought to be done with some sign of respect, to those that are present."

As I look at the life of our first president, I must ask myself what if he had looked at his educational status as a deterrent to his calling. His willingness to serve, led society to call him Father of His Country.

America God has a calling upon this great country that we live in, may we serve with integrity and firmness, as we walk through the challenging times of war and Covid.

JESUS A FRIEND OF THE SINNERS

LUKE 19:10

"For the son of Man came to seek and to save what was lost." Josephus a first century historian and military leader, spoke of the Pharisees as experts and expositors in the Jewish law. Pharisees received the good will of everyday people like you and me. They were educated, skilled to the point that they had a power to point out the law with assertiveness leaving out friendship and love.

We all have times in our lives that the ugly head of authoritarian law creeps into the lives of Christians. As office manager, I sat at my desk listening to an older staff member train a new employee. The method of teaching often included criticism and intimidation. The atmosphere alone would drive the staff away to seek other employment. Affirmation is a tool to build and will bring about success if used correctly.

Jesus expressed a rebuttal about the law of the Pharisees. In Luke 7-33-34: For John, the Baptist came neither eating or drinking wine, and you say, "He has a demon," The Son of Man came eating and drinking, and you say, "Here is a glutton and drunkard, a friend of the tax collectors and sinners. The law was of immense importance to the Pharisees therefore, paralyzing their efforts to be a winner. Our Lord wanted the Pharisees to be a friend of sinners.

Jesus reaches out to the marginal, the wounded, the liar, the thief, the adulteress, to bring hope amid a world that was broken in his time. His followers saw a man with a tender approach to win the loss. America, our Lord, and Savior needs you and me as we work to rebuild this great country that we live in.

RETURN TO SENDER

MALACHI 2:17

You have wearied the Lord with your words. Sometimes as Christians we tend to doubt God's word of protection for his people. Covid does not have control over God's people. We are victors and overcomers of all trials that come to our lives.

During these times of chaos, the news and media sends out messages of pandemonium to the subliminal minds of our nation. People have such a fear of the present situation, they find themselves depressed and broken. God promised his people peace, joy, love, and prosperity. The mind can easily be overtaken just like it did in the garden of Eden when Satan began to dialogue with Eve. Under the disguise of being wise as God, Satan led the couple from a utopia life to the fall of mankind.

The words of the woman who had the blood issue said, "If I can only touch the helm of his garment, I will be healed." She put aside the fact that she had spent all she had and still had a problem. Her words of affirmation brought healing to her body and soul.

When Goliath made demeaning gestors of laughter when he learned that David was his opponent in war, the words that he spoke never took residence within David. He took out his weapon anointed by the power of God and did what God called him to do. David spoke words of affirmation that led him to victory. In Hebrews 13: 5: Jesus said, "I will never leave you nor forsake you." These are words of affirmation to his people.

America, as we serve our Lord and Master, may words of doubt and fear disappear when we send subliminal messages back to the sender.

DIVINE FORGIVENESS

GENESIS 45:4-5

Then Joseph said to his brothers, "Come close to me." When they had done so, he said, "I am your brother Joseph, the one you sold into Egypt! And now, do not be distressed and do not be angry with yourselves for selling Me here, because it was to save lives that God sent me ahead of you.

At the age of six years old, Joseph traveled with his family to the land of Canaan. Jealously creeped its ugly head into the family that was anointed by God. Joseph was sold into slavery by his brothers at the age of seventeen. At the age of thirty he entered his place of employment in Pharoah's house. He lived 110 years of which ninety-three was spent in Egypt as a missionary that God divinely designed for his life.

This old archaic true story is often defined as a true example of divine forgiveness. He was sold at 17 years of age to slavery and did not see his family presumably until he was thirty-nine years old. Joseph's words "Come close to me, I am your brother Joseph," was the gateway of forgiveness that took place long before the meeting. His tender words do not be distressed and do not be angry with yourselves God sent me ahead of you to save lives.

As Christians, we sometimes hold on to hurts that deter the divine plan that God has for our lives. There are hurts that certainly justify emotional pain, but we must forgive. Joseph's life had many emotional turns, family, prison, and then to second in command in the house of Pharoah. He left an example of true forgiveness.

As we face these uncertain times in America, let us be reminded that God's way is always right. He will never leave us or forsake us.

HONOR THE DIGNITY OF OTHERS

PROVERBS 3:3-4

Let love and faithfulness never leave you; bind them around your neck, write them on the tablet of your heart. Then you will win favor and a good name in the sight of God and man.

During my youth, I would often drive to a church camp to have Christian fellowship. The cabin I stayed in was approximately six feet by six foot in size. A ray of light would peak through the window as the cobwebs glistened in the corner. When you sat on the bed, it felt as if rocks were tucked somewhere in the mattress. As a young person that did not matter to me, I loved every moment of my summer retreat at camp.

Each morning the bell would ring signifying that the morning service was about to begin. I would set the alarm and quietly get out of bed so I would not miss one moment with the dear saints of God. I would listen to the stories of wisdom, healing, and instructions that as a youth I needed. There was such a reverence within my heart for the old and wiser adults that paved the way before me.

As I sat in the sanctuary one morning, people within the audience began to speak one by one expressing their love for the Lord and how God so wonderfully saved them. The authentic words of these dear saints have permeated my life from youth to old age. God gives us these moments as a reminder that when his people serve him it spills out to others giving hope and peace.

America as we face these troublesome times, remember you cannot put a price tag as we reach out with God's love and touch the heart of others.

SEEKING COUNSEL

Psalm 32:8-9

I will instruct you and teach you in the way you should go; I will counsel you and watch over you. Do not be like the horse or the mule, which have the understanding but must be controlled by bit and bridle.

The phone rang one afternoon and the voice on the other end was a young lady that I had met and briefly known for about six months. Her voice quivered as she spoke of her dilemma that had consumed her personal life. As she spoke of her troubles, it was as if she was waiting for a quick fix for her situation. As I listen to her speak, she had knowledge of the word of God, however her will was like a horse that needed to be controlled by a bit and bridle. This dear lady listened to the inter voice that sent her down the wrong path. The ramifications of her choice brought great sorrow into her life as well as to her family.

As Christian, we sometimes make choices that grieve the heart of God. Obedience is hard when we want to manage the path that God has designed for our lives. An example was given of a great man of God that staged his own path with he engaged in a relationship with Bathsheba. King David sought forgiveness but could have ended his sorrow through his obedience.

America, let us hold on to the word of God and take instructions from our Lord during the tough times. The bible says he will counsel and watch over us when we look for resolution as we walk through these troublesome times.

A QUIET PLACE OF REST

Mark 30:31

Come with me by yourselves to a quiet place and get some rest.

It has been a tough time for America as we face the challenges that Covid brings coupled with Ukraine war. The senseless war has taken the lives of so many, destroyed cities and business stunting the welfare and financial stability of Ukraine country. Tears of anguish and pain radiates the hearts of Ukraine as they work through the chaos of war.

For the past two years, I have found that if I find a quiet place to pray that it is comforting to know that truly God is working in the lives of our country as we walk through the challenging times. Many days as I kneel to pray, I feel his presence in such an authentic way. Although my heart is heavy, God brings an enduring peace that makes me look forward to my daily quiet time with him.

Apostle Paul wrote that we should talk to God about everything. That means being honest about our hidden concerns. I can just see Paul as he walked through his own pain there were times, I am sure that he fell prostate before God when society made his past life his future. In Philippians 3:13: Paul said, "Brothers, I do not consider myself yet to have taken hold of it, but one thing I do know is forgetting what is behind and straining toward what is ahead." was imperative to this dear man of God.

America a quiet place and getting some rest will heal the inter soul of mankind as we walk through the tough times.

FILL OUR HEARTS WITH NEW WINE

JOHN 2:4-7

"Dear woman, why do you involve me?" Jesus replied, "My time has not yet come." His mother said to the servant, "Do whatever he tells you," Nearby stood six stone water jars, the kind used for ceremonial washing, each holding from twenty to thirty gallons. Jesus said to the servants, "Fill the jars with water." so they filled them to the brim. Then he told them, "Now draw some out and take it to the master of the banquet."

I can just see Jesus as he entered the wedding feast, looking for a place where his notoriety diminished as he mixed through the crowd. The weddings in those days would often last several days, after the third day of the wedding, all the wine was gone. The human element shows up in Jesus when he said, "Dear woman, why do you involve me?" As I read this passage, I could not help but think how we as Christians are asked to serve at times and we just want to rest as Jesus did. None the less, he listened to the instructions of his mother and had the servants fill the water pots to the brim.

As the servants drew from the pots there was a divine wine representing the blood of Jesus as the Messiah that was served to the master of ceremonies. Notice how Jesus did this great miracle in such a way that only those behind the scenes could see the authenticity of his work.

America, God can fill our pots with new wine that strengthens the soul as we walk through tough times of war and pandemic. When humanity called upon Jesus, he set aside his own personal feelings to serve. God has the same intentions for America if we let him fill our hearts with New Wine as we work together to bring hope to America.

QUITTING IS NOT AN OPTION

1 CORINTHIANS 15:58

Therefore, my dear brothers, stand firm. Let nothing move you. Always give yourselves fully to the work of the Lord because you know that your labor in the Lord is not in vain.

As a young mother at the age of twenty-five years of age, words were spoken to me that almost consumed my life and stability as a Christian. As I tried to dissect the words, discouragement filled my heart wondering if I would ever overcome the cruel dialogue that came from the offender. Late that evening as I prayed, I ask God to help me understand why someone would speak so harshly. As I placed my head on the pillow that night, I fell into a deep sleep. My dream placed me on a road that was steep and hard to climb. The road did not level out giving ease to the climb, it was a struggle. As I continued the climb, there were times that I was on my knees crawling, but I never stopped going upward. As I was approaching the end of the road, I could hear such beautiful music like no music I have ever heard before. There was a large gate that captured the scene of events. I approached the gate to see what was inside, it opened gently and there stood the Lord to welcome me home.

God gave me affirmation that serving him would have many challenges and that I must continue to climb through discouragements. Paul knew something about the challenges that the church would face when he wrote the letter to the Corinthians. The city of Corinth was a wealthy trading center and many of the people were living sinful complacent lives. Paul wanted to inform them to keep on climbing upward leaving out complacency and sin.

America, we must work diligently during the discouraging times and continue to climb upward as we serve the Lord.

SPREAD THE GOOD NEWS

MATTHEW 9:27-29

As Jesus went on from there, two blind men followed him, calling out, "Have mercy on us, Son of David!" When he had gone indoors, the blind men came to him, and he asked them, "Do you believe that I am able to do this?" "Yes Lord," they replied. Then he touched their eyes and said, "According to your faith will it be done to you."

As Jesus touched the eyes of the two blind men, "I can just see the two of them jumping with joy that their sight had been restored. Jesus instructed them not to tell anyone, but they could not contain themselves. Jesus had just performed a miracle in their lives, and the instructions of Jesus took back seat to their joy. I imagine the people in the room was taken back by two men that was not afraid to announce his name. When Jesus said "Do you believe?" "Their response was, "Yes Lord, we believe."

As we serve the Lord during these troubled times that America and the entire world faces, may we never be afraid to associate ourselves with the God of Abraham, Isaac, and Jacob. I have been in situations where when the word of God is mentioned the room becomes silently awkward. For the blind men, nothing could hold them back from praising God. They were blind and now they could see.

As I sat in a prayer session the leader asks each of us to give a synopsis of born-again Christian. A lady within the group's definition said it is a deep profound relationship with Jesus Christ. America, God desires intimacy as we serve him during these trouble times.

OUR LORD WEPT THREE TIMES

HEBREWS 5:7

During the days of Jesus' life on earth, he offered up prayers and petitions with loud cries and tears to the one who could save him from death, and he was heard because of his reverent submission.

The act of obedience exemplified by Jesus in Hebrew 5:7 was hard to say the least. He knew he was going to have to sacrifice his life for humanity as he talked with God. He cried with loud tears to his Heavenly father yet showing great reverence and submission. His human mind yet divine, took him to the road of Calvary that pierced his side and put thorns upon his head. As he contemplated his death and resurrection obedience was at the forefront.

The human emotions that Jesus showed in John 11:35, when Mary fell at the Lord's feet telling him that her brother Lazarus had died. She said Lord if you had only been here my brother would not have died. Overwhelmed with compassion Jesus Wept and fulfilled his call to humanity when he told Lazarus to come out of the tomb and take off his grave clothes. The glory of our Lord and Savior was exalted that day as a reminder the deity of Christ.

As Jesus approached the nearing of his crucifixion. He approached the city of Jerusalem and wept. He had a deep profound desire to see them grow as a Christian when he said. "If they had only known what would bring them peace." Tears fell from our Lord's eyes.

God has a plan for this great country that we live in. May we always take instructions from our Lord and Savior, as we serve him. Obedience cost nothing but the rewards are great.

SPIRITUAL AWAKENING

ROMANS 14:1

Accept him whose faith is weak, without passing judgement on disputable matters.

My entire life, I have attended church each Sunday. It was just something that brought solace to my soul. I cannot remember a time that I did not want to go. Although, I thought it was a safe place to be, there was apathy among the saints of God. The early church often used criticism as a tool to restore the new members to the ecological standards of the church.

Inviting people to church was something that God laid upon my heart. There were times that God opened the door of opportunity and someone within the church closed it. As I walked into the church one morning, one of the older saints approached a newcomer about the attire, the door closed that day for the dear family, and they never came back.

The Pungi instrument is used to charm the snakes. It is also theorized that it is used to take people to a half-conscious state. The Church can so easily fall into an authoritarian approach leaving out the human element that Jesus so instilled within the body of Christ. The twenty third Psalms says he anoints our head with Oil protecting us from the snares that life often brings.

May we as the family of God use methods to restore and build the Church. Jesus is a notable example of interpersonal skills used to win the lost. I loved how he spoke to Zacchaeus the tax collector when he said, I am going to your home today. It was an individualized outreach to Zacchaeus. Let us reflect during this great pandemic the example that Jesus the Church.

LET THE WEAK SAY I AM STRONG

JOEL 3:10

Let the weak say I am strong. Joel was a prophet with a description of what a severe locus pandemic literally and spiritually could do to the land. The example was to inform the people of Israel to take note of what happened when Pharoah's disobedience affected his people.

As Joel spoke, he had knowledge of what the Locus could do when Pharoah would not let his people go. Exodus 10: 1-3, states, let my people go, so they may worship me. If you refuse, I will bring locusts into your country tomorrow. They will devour what little you have left.

If you looked at the passage metaphorically, Joel was a prophet that was seeking restoration for God's people. He warned them of a future day that God will judge his people. Joel 1:6-7: Says, "A nation has invaded my land, powerful and without number; it has teeth of a lion the fangs of a lioness, it has laid waste my vines and ruined my fig trees. It has stripped off their bark and thrown it away, leaving their branches white."

As we face the turbulent waters that a pandemic brings, God wants his people to turn back to him. He wants us to recognize him as almighty God that will sustain when the water of life is muddy. When war, sickness, death is on the horizon, he wants us to be strong as Joel said, "Let the weak say I am strong."

America we are strong when we hold on to the strong arms of the Lord Jesus Christ. Joel is depicting words of wisdom to repent and turn back to the God of Israel.

LITTLE IS MUCH WHEN GOD IS IN IT

2 CORINTHIANS 6:1-2

As God's fellow workers we urge you not to receive God's grace in vain. For he says, "In the time of my favor I heard you, and in the day of salvation I will help you.

There may be times that God assigns you a task that seems so mundane and of no value. There is a song called Little is Much when God is in it. One of the verses says, "Does the place you are called to labor seem too small and little known? It is great if God is in it, and he will not forget his own. It may that you are asked to clean the church. It is a behind the scenes job, but little did you know that someone would come in the church seeking counsel and you led them to the Lord. That assignment was little and became big because God was there.

I knew of a teenager that had many opportunities to reach out to people at work. She learned of a family that needed financial help and took groceries to the store front apartment. As the young lady walked in there was a mother and five children. The two bags of groceries could not feed this dear family in human eyes, but in God's eyes he fed a multitude with five loaves and two fish. As the story goes, a deep profound relationship took place with this dear family when little was much when God was in it. Church attendance became a part of the family's life.

Proverbs 16:3 says, commit to the Lord whatever you do, and your plans will be successful. America we as a Nation can help those that are in need during these troubled times. Big tasks are great and little ones invaluable. God sees them all as we bring healing to our nation.

WAR CRY FROM GOD'S PEOPLE

1 SAMUEL 17:45

Then David said to the Philistines, "You come to me with a sword and with a spear and with a Javelin, but I come to you in the name of the Lord of host, the God of the armies of Israel, whom you have defied.

The dynamic divine anointment that Jehovah God place upon David's life could not be diminished by his oldest brother. As Jesse the father of David sent him down to view the battle between Israel and the Philistines he went under the appointment of almighty God. Eliab the oldest brother heard David speaking with the men and his anger pivoted when he said. "Why have you come down here?" And with whom did you leave those few sheep. I can just see Eliab's face as he said, "I know how pretentious and conceited you are you came here to watch the battle. The words of discouragement did not deter David from what God had called him to do.

As Christians we have those times that God calls us to a specific task. The tool that we have may be limited but when God sanctions our work nothing can stop the divine work of almighty. The out of the ordinary sling shot was anointed. Assurance within David's soul spoke loudly when he said, I come to you in the name of the Lord. David obeyed his father Jesse as he took on the challenges of his limited resources and discouragements of his older brother.

America, we are God's people, and we must seek the will of Almighty God. If our resources are limited, God can sanction a divine resolution for our great country and families. David dumped the negative and picked up the anointed tool of restoration. May we use his example as we walk through this tough time of war and Covid.

WORDS OF AFFIRMATION

PROVERBS 21:23

He who guards his mouth, and his tongue keeps himself from calamity. The tongue is a small member of the body and can be deadly if not controlled.

A colleague of mine shared a story about her going back to school to get her master's in business. She said that when she entered the room and the professors looked at her that the professor told her that she would never make it in her class. She said, "Well, me being the good student that I am and you being the great teacher you are, I will get my masters with no problem. My friend and colleague did just that. She beat the odds of defeat projected by the professor. She went on to start her own business and did quite well.

There are two ways we can react to criticism; we can let it make us angry or we can learn from it. The young lady expressed her anger and she also learned from it. Ole Bull the violinist wanted desperately to play with notoriety. In Italy, a Milan newspaper critic wrote: He is an untrained musician. If he be a diamond, he is certainly in the rough and unpolished. Ole Bull was offered a space in the New York Herald to answer his critics. He said, "I think it best that they write against me, and I play against them."

As we go through these tough times, may we as leaders challenge ourselves to use words of affirmation leaving out politics and working together for the good of our country. Proverbs 3:27 says, "Do not withhold good from those who deserve it, when it is in your power to do so."

I WANT TO GO WITH YOU

JOHN 21:17

The third time he said to him, "Simon, son of John, do you truly love me?" Peter was hurt because Jesus asked him the third time, "Do you love me?" He said, "Lord you know all things, you know that I love you."

After the resurrection, the bewilderment of his disciples left them feeling hopeless. I am sure thoughts went through their minds as they pondered the death and resurrection of Christ. Peter was at the forefront of guilt and shame bringing condemnation to his heart and soul. As Peter examined himself, I am sure that he was unsure of his standing with the Lord. When the Lord appeared to the disciples on the sea of Galilee after the resurrection, it was a place that they were all familiar with. He came to them as if to say, I want to go with you always. He did not look at the sin of Peter, he looked at a man that was strong, fearful, and vulnerable fearing for his own life.

There came a time that Peter was completely sold out to the cause of our Lord and Savior. In Luke 22:32-33, depicts the Lord telling Peter that he has been praying for him and he wants him to strengthen his brothers. As Peter dialogued with Jesus, he said Lord, I am ready to go with you to prison and to death. The Lord never looked at Peters sin, he reached into the recesses of his heart with tenderness as if to say, I can see a man of great faith and fortitude to carry the gospel.

As we face the many challenges ahead with war in Ukraine and Covid permeating our world, Jesus says, I want to go with you during these challenging times just like I did with Peter. God will forgive the sins of America and bring power and peace to our Nation.

GOD USES THE INEVITABLE

GALATIANS 1:13

For you have heard of my earlier way of life in Judaism, how intensely I persecuted the Church of God and tried to destroy it.

Saul is a masculine name of Hebrew origin depicting strength among the Jewish nation as king. On the Damascus Road upon his conversions the Lord Jesus commissioned him to take the gospel to the Gentiles. He gave Saul a new name Paul, meaning little and small. One would wonder why God chose a man of such hostility to lead his people. He persecuted and denigrated the church using his advanced years in Judaism as a tool to execute the traditions of his forefathers.

God saw something in this man that Satan was using to harm the church and destroyed the weapon on the road to Damascus. There is no power in Satan in the presence of the Lord. In first Corinthians 1:15:3: For what I have received I passed on to you as of first importance: that Christ died for our sins according to the Scriptures, that he was buried, that he was raised on the third day. Paul's acknowledgement that Jesus was Lord broke the weapon of persecution when he accepted the great commission of Jesus Christ.

As Christians, we are commissioned to carry the gospel to the entire world as God gives us moments of opportunity. Many years ago, I ask the Lord to give me an opportunity to serve in my place of employment. I did a simple invite to church and the whole family came and attended church until my dear friend passed away to meet the Lord. As our world faces the challenges ahead, may we be commissioned for his cause when God gives us the opportunity to serve.

REBUILDING AMERICA

ZECHARIAH 4:9

The hands of Zerubbabel have laid the foundation of this temple; his hand will also complete it. Then you will know that the Lord Almighty has sent me to you.

God appointed Zerubbabel to complete the temple for his people. Obstacles was at the forefront as he waded through the logistical paperwork that construction often causes. When the enemies of Judah and Benjamin heard that Zerubbabel was building the temple, they asked that they be part of the plan. As Zerubbabel responded by saying you may not have a part with us in building the temple as we are building it alone for Yahweh, the God of Israel. Legend has it that it may have taken three years, but other sources depicts that it took much longer. Yes, the temple was built because God instructed Zerubbabel to lay the foundation and to complete it.

The significance of this great leader was of much importance for God's people. As he approached many trials during his leadership, he never wavered or gave up on the call that God had for his life. Perseverance was a strong characteristic that God had given him and therefore chose this man to conduct his plan for Israel. He was going to build the temple for God's people.

The great pandemic that America has faced during the last two years calls for leadership that can throw out the plum line and persevere as we rebuild our nation through war and Covid. God has a plan, and he wants his people to hold on to his promises leaving out fear and pandemonium as our country heals.

A FRIEND OF THE SINNERS

LUKE 15:1-2

Now the tax collectors and sinners were all gathering around to hear him. The Pharisees and the teachers of the law muttered, this man welcomes sinners and eats with them.

Jesus was like a magnet that pulled people into his circle of love and affections. He never looked at the social ambience of his surroundings. His mission was to save the lost and heal the land. The spiritual immaturity of the Pharisees and teachers that gathered around him certainly was not something that our Lord was proud of. Jesus lived by example showing the world the importance of being a friend to the sinners.

In raising children, we as parents go to great lengths to restore a child when we see their path going in the wrong direction. Jesus gave examples to his people when he compared vulnerable sheep that had wondered away from the place of security in the story of the lost sheep. Luke 15-1-4. He reached the marginal, the broken, adulterous, liar, the sinner. He spoke words of affirmation and love in Matthew 11:28. Come to me all you who are weary and burdened, and I will give you rest.

Jesus made it clear that he came to save the lost and that the rank in the societal arena. would never be a deterrent as he led people to hope and eternal life.

May the Lord bless us as we face our challenges to restore our nation. Let us be willing to have the spirit of Christ and be a friend to those as Jesus did. He was a loyal friend of the sinners.

JESUS COMMANDED

Matthew 7:5

You hypocrite, first take the plank out of your own eye, and then you will see clearly to remove the speck from your brother's eye.

As the young lady entered the church one morning, her hair was red mixed with black streaks. The ring in her nose jumped out at you as if to say look at me I am beautiful. The black attire and boots brough attention and turned the heads of the parishioners as she passed by. It was as if the church did not know how to respond to a dress code that was different than the traditional church. She was young and needed someone to love her where she was and not judge her by their internal values. As I approached her, I told her I was glad she came. Her eyes smiled as if to say, I am glad I came too.

I have a necklace that I sometimes wear that has a little book and as you open the book it says, Mother Theresa said, "when you judge people, you do not have time to love them." Jesus was remarkable at loving the world looking past judgmental walls of condemnation.

Matthew 11: 28-30

He said come to me, all you who are weary and heavy laden. Our Lord's eyes were focused on the soul of man not his appearance and demeanor. His mission was to bring hope and peace leaving judgmental dialogue out of the equation.

Although church was my lifeline, I saw areas that we as the family of God could improve. Our Lord reached out past every boundary never looking at the external giving the heart and soul his full attention. May we as a nation and church love with the eyes of our Lord as we come face to face with challenging times in America and our Nation.

SUBSTAINING THE WEARY

ISAIAH 50:4

The Sovereign Lord has given me an instructed tongue, to know the word that sustains the weary. He wakens me morning by morning, wakens my ear to listen like one being taught.

As we rise in them morning, may we take a moment just to say the above scripture aloud to remind us to say words of wisdom and hope to our family, work associates and encounters as we face our day. There is an old cliché that says, "We make a living by what we get, and a life by what we give." The gift of encouragement will lift the spirits of those we meet daily. The instructed tongue will listen and sustain the weary.

The morning supervisor approached a young lady with demeaning words of criticism as she approached her department. The employee dropped her head as if she had committed a crime. It was as if she wanted to become invisible behind a scrim of fog. The work ethic of the young lady was incredible, the demeaning words changed the countenance of the young lady and she eventually moved on to another position that gave credibility that was well deserved.

The word of God instructs us how to use words of kindness in our daily lives. The tongue can debilitate the church, home, and workplace if we are not careful. We must be vigilant daily pondering over the words that come out of our mouth. Nations, people, and leadership will flourish when words are constructive tagged with a positive twist.

LEARN HOW TO BE CHILDLIKE

MATTHEW 18:3

And he said: "I tell you the truth unless you change and become like little children, you will never enter the kingdom of heaven."

The flowers in the spring were at full blossom. Daffodils of yellow spread its petals as if to say, it is spring. My morning walk with all the radiant colors seem to fill my soul with the presence of the Lord. He created this wonderful world that we live in for his people to enjoy. As I continued my walk, there was a gentleman across the road with three children. Good morning, ma'am, have a lovely day today a little voice spoke. As I looked up, the little child dressed in a pink dress with ribbons to match, brought a ray of sunshine to my heart. It was as if God greeted me.

There was a reason Jesus left this scripture as a guideline for humanity. Children will play, they will fight, they will cry but, in the end, they have such a way of leaving out the noise of the world. The little miss stroller brough a ray of sunshine in my soul that will long be remembered.

Sometimes in this world we meet trouble in the churches, the home and family. In 1 Corinthians 14: 20, it says, Brothers, stop thinking like children about evil be infants, but in your thinking be adults.

As we face uncertainties, may we use these two passages of scripture as a guideline to model our lives. Jesus loves us so much that he wants us to be more childlike in spirit and adult like as we face the challenges that life often brings.

LEAVING HER PAST BEHIND

RUTH 1:15

And she said, see your sister-in-law has gone back to her people and to her gods; return after your sister-in-law.

There was just something about the God of Israel that Naomi introduced her daughters-in-law, Orpah and Ruth to that penetrated deep within the soul of Ruth. As Naomi, instructed them to go home to their families' words of kindness flowed from the lips of this dear grieving lady when she said, "May the Lord show kindness to you, as you have shown to your dead and to me. May each of you find rest in the home of another husband.

An ancient West Semitic deity name Che mosh, was revered by the Moabites as their supreme God. There was just something about the God that Naomi introduced Ruth to, that filled her soul with delight and honor. As Orpah returned to her homeland, Ruth stood firm letting go of her past teaching and clinging to the God of Israel. As the story goes, God cared enough about this dear lady that he gave her another husband and she bore a son named Obed that was the father of Jesse, the father of David in the line of Christ.

Obedience by Ruth a Moabite by birth, has so many factors of success to the God of Israel. She would not relent regardless of the persuasion of Naomi to go back to her people and her God. Our Lord and Savior came from the line of Jesse bringing hope to a broken world. God uses humanity to fulfill his purpose for a fallen world. May we take a stand as we face challenging times as Ruth did. She had lost everything, and restoration came through obedience bringing hope and peace through the birth of Jesus Christ.

CIRCLE OF LOVE

PHILIPPIANS 4:6-7

Do not be anxious about anything, but in everything, by prayer and petition with thanksgiving, present your requests to God.

As I raised my children, one of the things that sticks in my mind was the circle of love. From time to time, I would draw that circle on their arm and when they would leave, I would draw the circle in the air signifying my love for them. These were such special moments of sincere love that words could not express.

Honi was a Jewish Scholar of the first century. He was labeled as a circle maker. During a severe drought he drew a circle and placed himself within it and began to pray fervently for God to send rain upon the earth. Honi spoke to God as a son would speak to his father. When he prayed for rain and God did not answer, he talked with God persistently and drew a prayer circle insisting that he was not going to move until God had pity for his people. As it began to rain violently, he said, "Not for such rain have I prayed, but for rain of goodwill, blessing, and graciousness. Honi's prayer became specific.

As I write this devotion, our world is upside down. Our families face so much uncertainty financially and spiritually as Covid takes the lives of so many. May we each draw that circle of love around our families and world creating a prayer circle with unwavering faith until God answers prayer. America we can do this. We can talk with God as a child talking to his parents staying inside the circle of love until prayer is answered. God honors a man when man includes him inside his spiritual arena.

A COMMANDMENT WITH A PROMISE

EPHESIAN 6:1-2

Children obey your parents in the Lord, for this is right. 'Honor your father and mother" which is the first commandment with a promise.

Throughout Asia, respect for the elderly is what sociologist describe as filial piety. Their goal is to revere the imperative adhering to respect and honor.

As I walked the streets of Mexico City, whole families would be walking together showing their loyalty as a family to the world. Mexican family culture holds extraordinarily strong family ties and is deeply rooted to their traditions. One of their core beliefs is that Unity brings Strength. As I took a boat ride, I saw entire families out for the day cooking as they strolled through the waters. Their jesters of love spilled out to Americans that passed by. As we strolled, there were beautiful flowers of many colors. The families had their own barbeque spreading the sweet aroma to the winds of the earth as they strolled. Life was simply beautiful.

I watched as the young men, put their arms around their elderly parents with honor and pride. This is what the scripture means when it says to honor your father and mother. Our American society is lax in reverence to parents. Children and young adults in America will often circumvent their emotions of respect and honor with weakness rather than strength.

God gave us this great commandment by Paul as he was imprisoned with a promise saying, "It will go well with you, and you will have long life. The core values of family and respect will bring peace to America as we walk through tuff times.

UNIQUELY MADE FOR GOD'S PURPOSE

1 CORINTHIANS 4:2

Now it is required that those who have been given a trust must prove faithful.

In the first century AD, Apostle John was exiled to the island of Patmos. His crime was carrying the gospel to the world around him. God uniquely made John to bring peace and joy to a broken world.

As John was placed on the Island of Patmos, he was placed among people of crime by the Roman Emperor Titus Flavius in 95 AC. It is interesting that John did not let his place of employment deter him from the work God made him to do. It was as if he told God, "You put me here and I am going to make the best of it." In Revelation 1:9: John, both your brother and companion in tribulation was on the island that is called Patmos for the word of God and for the testimony of Jesus Christ. John had firsthand as a disciple of Jesus Christ that faced human emotions that included being tired, sad, hungry, and loving yet he never wavered to reach the lost in whatever situation he met.

America has faced trials and life has been full of uncertainties during Covid. When life does not go along with our original plans may we adjust with a positive attitude as John did. John was an Author, Theologian, Fisherman, and Apostle. The Lord had trust in this dear apostle to conduct the narrative events of his ministry that would bring life and hope to a fallen world.

May we as Americans never let our surroundings be a deterrent to the unique person that God designed us to be. Our Lord designed us to be a servant during the good and tough times of life. Let us do it.

GOD'S PLAN FOR HIS PEOPLE

OBADIAH 1:4

Though you soar like the eagle and make your nest among the stars, from there I will bring you down, declares the Lord.

The prophecy of Obadiah, that God's people would be protected and that the wicked nation of Edom would fall was the focus of this prophet. His words were few but profound and prophetic. As the Edomites plundered and invaded Jerusalem several times, Obadiah encouraged Israel that God saw and would deliver his people even though the circumstances at the time seemed dim.

As insurmountable challenges face our country, with politics fighting for what each party considers as truth, may we all take a moment to remember that God loves each of us and wants to bring blessings to our world. When God gave Obadiah the prophetic knowledge regarding Edom, he said, "Though you nest among the stars, from there I will bring you down." He warns Edom of hypocrisy saying they will not be heard of no more after the fall and destruction of Jerusalem. One might ask themselves what if Edom had adhered to the plan that God had originally planned for their lives.

As we work together to restore our country may we build a wall of peace within the system of our government that is not defined by one political party. We all have a place at God's table of grace, let us work in unity to restore hope to this wonderful world that God has given to his people.

FINE OIL OF PROTECTION

PSALM 92:10:

You have exalted my horn like that of a wild ox; fine oil has been poured upon me:

Psalm 92:10 is a short powerful declaration of God's mighty power and strength. The introduction to Psalms says that King David was thought to be the author of one hundred of the 150. Assuming David is the protagonist of this verse certainly he had firsthand to great trials and tribulation of which he did not know how to manage.

Proclamation of hope came when the author spoke words of exultation as he tried to make sense of the pandemonium in his daily arena. As David faced Goliath the giant in his youthful life, he may have been around five foot tall. Commentaries say that Goliath was between seven to eleven feet in size. I can just see David as he quoted the above scripture when he said you have exalted my horn like that of a wild ox and I have been anointed with a fine oil of supernatural power that only comes from God to his people. Defeat was not an option for David.

America as we face the challenges that Covid has brought to this country, may we take a deep breath and let God anoint our heads with the oil of strength even when the inevitable is at the forefront. I am sure as David viewed the giant; thoughts of fear entered his mind. God instructed him how to oversee his fear with just a few stones and a slingshot. Obedience wiped out the fear and he stood tall in faith as he obeyed the God of Israel.

We as American have access to the same God that David built his life upon. The oil is God's way of saying that I love you and anoint you with my oil that will deliver you from harm.

THE WISDOM OF DEBORAH

JUDGES 4:8

Barak said to her, "If you go with me, I will go, but if you do not go with me, "I won't."

Israel sinned and God allowed them to be turned over to the king in Canaan. The commander of the army was Sisera and had nine hundred iron chariots and used his power cruelly oppressing the Israelites. It was at this time that Israel cried out for help from Jehovah God of Israel.

Deborah was a busy woman judging between Ramah and Bethel in the country of Ephraim. She was a Prophetess that was led by prayer and supplication. Deborah instructed Barak to take ten thousand men of Naphtali and Zebulun to Mount Tabor and she would lure Jabin's army to Kishon River and give the army into his hands. Fear of approaching the army alone, Barak said to her, "If you go with me, I will go." Fear took the place of faith costing Barak his place of honor.

Deborah spoke honestly to Barak when she said, "I will go with you but because of the way you have gone about this, the honor will not be yours, it will be in the hands of a woman. This dear lady is an example of a woman that prayed, seeking wisdom from the almighty God for the Israeli people.

As we work together to restore our country, let us consider being a Deborah seeking wisdom that only God can give during a crisis. He loves America and his people. May we honor him today with our obedience and make America Strong.

THE BUDDED STAFF

NUMBERS 17:8

The next day Moses entered the Tent of the Testimony and saw that Aaron's staff, which stood for the house of Levi, had not only sprouted but had budded, blossomed, and produced almonds.

In the book of Exodus, Moses and Aaron led Israel out of bondage so they could serve and worship their God. When Pharoah decided that he was not going to free the enslaved Israelites, God sent the plagues to show the world the false Gods of Egypt was not a match to the God of Abraham, Isaac, and Jacob.

All the miracles that took place after Israel was delivered, seemed to pale at times when they stepped outside of God's plans. The specific instructions were written for Israel about the Manna that he supplied daily. He told them not to save it that he would supply food daily as they needed it. They began to save it and it turned to worms. It was as if Israel did not know what to do with themselves after their release from Pharoah. Disobedience limited those that entered the promise land that God had for his people.

As Moses presented the twelve staffs to the ancestral tribes, the only one that bloomed was the staff of Arron. Although Israel sinned, the significance of the budded staff was God's way of saying I still believe in you so go forward with what I called you to do.

As we face extreme difficulties in our world through Covid, may we seek out resolution by obedience to the word of God by making good decision that will bring hope to our nation. As a little girl once said, "God's love is defined by a world with his big arms around it."

JESUS DEPLORED RELIGIOUS SYSTEMS

MATTHEW 8:3

Jesus reached out his hand and touched the man, "I am willing," he said. "Be clean." Immediately he was cured of his leprosy.

There were times that Jesus raised the eyebrows of humanity when he stepped across the religious proclamation that society considered during his ministry. As the leopard knelt before Jesus this day, the Lord said "I am willing to make you clean." When the Centurion called upon Jesus to heal his servant, Jesus replied, "I will go." The Centurion officer in the army of ancient Rome replied, "Lord I do not deserve to have you under my roof, just say the word and my servant will be healed."

I can just see the astonishment on the face of Jesus as he marvels at the faith of the Centurion. Matthew 8:10: I tell you the truth, I have not found such great faith." The words of affirmation certainly will live forever as we break down the division within our Religious System. Do you see how Jesus reached out to the unclean leopard and then in the same chapter he reached out to the distinguished Centurion. The societal walls of distinction were an example that Jesus wanted his people to adhere breaking down the walls that divide us. The woman at the well in John 4: said. "Sir I am a Samaritan woman, and you are a Jew and Jews do not associate with Samaritans. Jesus reached out and gave her living water.

As America faces the obstacles during the pandemic, may we reach out our hand in fellowship across the political regime working together as we bring healing to our Nation. I can envision the Samaritan leaving the well that day with inter peace as she said "Sir give me this water so that I may not thirst again. Jesus brought hope.

A MIRACLE AWAITS AMERICA

JOHN 11:14

Lazarus is dead, and for your sake I am glad I was not there, so that you may believe. Let us go to him.

When Mary and Martha sent word to the Lord that Lazarus was dead the devastation of his loss was overwhelming. As they spoke the words to Jesus their grief was exemplified in the voice and soul of the sisters when they said, "Lord the one you love is sick." One might ask, why Jesus stayed two more days before he made his journey back to Bethany. In John 11: Jesus said, "This sickness will not end in death." Visual healing was not in place yet, but Jesus knew that he would heal in his time.

When Mary reached the place where Jesus was, she fell at his feet and said, "Lord if you had been here, he would not have died. Every emotion possible was visible and the scripture says the grief of Mary and Martha showed the human element when Jesus Wept. Jesus knew full well that he was going to raise Lazarus from the dead even though he was dead for four days. The inevitable was at the forefront when Jesus told Martha, "Did I not tell you that if you believed you would see the glory of God."

The same miracles that Jesus performed during the biblical times are forever true today. Our nation is overwhelmed with fear and pandemonium as we fight the deadly disease of Covid. God is here we just must reach out and put no time limits on how he heals our country. He loves this great nation and weeps at the sorrow that we are facing. May we reach out in fellowship and believe the biblical principles that Jesus spoke to Mary and Martha. Jesus loved them and he loves us. Healing is coming as God works out his plan.

NEVER LET GO OF YOUR INNER CHILD

MATTHEW 18:1-2

At that time, the disciples came to Jesus and asked, "Who is the greatest in the kingdom of heaven." He called a little child and had him stand among them, and he said, "I tell you the truth, unless you change and become like little children, you will never enter the kingdom of heaven.

The doorbell rang one afternoon and with hesitance I peeked around the wall to see if I could visualize the body standing at my door. I went down the steps and quickly opened the door and there stood before me a little guy of about three- and one-half foot dressed in a cub scout uniform. As he looked into my eyes, he said, "I am raising money for the scouts and for three dollars you can have two Beef Jerky's or mix them with spicy ones. His little face was simply radiant. After my purchase, he said, "Do you know who I am?" As I examined his little face, eyes and hair, two years of Covid robbed me from recognition of the young lad. His eyes lit up as he said, "I am Matthew the little boy down the street that you use to talk with." Excusing my forgetfulness and recognition problem, I explained it away by his long hair. Oh, he said, "I am letting it grow and will donate it to the cancer society." Little Matthew was the epitome of what Jesus spoke about.

As we caught up with the past two years, I ask him about his school and his grades. He said, "I got straight A's ma'am with a glow that only success will bring. "As we dialogued, I told him that his name meant a Gift from God and I know that he will add so much to the lives of others with his beautiful spirit of love and affection. As Jesus told his disciples, this is what he meant. Our Lord wants America to work together as a team to bring hope and healing to our Nation.

YOU HAVE A PROMISE LAND

PHILIPPIANS 4:19

And my God will meet all your needs according to his glorious riches in Christ Jesus.

Israel had many complaints after they exited the land of Egypt under the direction of Pharoah. Miracle after miracle was performed right in front of their eyes. The Red Sea parting, Manna from heaven the Budded staff and the miraculous miracles seemed to fade in the distance when life got tough. They continue to complain as they made their journey and many of the Israelite spent forty years wandering in the wilderness. It was not just the land where Israel would live it was the promised Inheritance to God's chosen people.

I personally feel that we all have a Promise Land within our life's arena. When God looks down observing his people working and striving for the betterment of our country, leaving out their own personal agenda a Promise Land of Hope and peace will come to our nation. The promise land is a gift to us, and it was a gift to Israel. Complaining brought 40 years of delay to God's promise. May we not do a repeat as we face this great pandemic wandering in the unknown.

God's great promise is that he will always be with us. His timing is perfect. Our Lord is always good, and he is always watching over his people. In the end as we serve him in obedience and stop getting in his way, he will show us how victorious our lives can be.

As we seek wisdom and instructions from our Lord, may we let the walls of intimidation fall as we obey. God wants to take us away from the wilderness bringing hope to a hurting world. America, we can do it.

ARE YOU THIRSTY?

JOHN 7:37

If anyone is thirsty, let him come to me and drink. Whoever believes in me, as the Scripture has said, streams of living water will flow from within him.

In the world that we live in, there is no escaping our differences. God uniquely made us in his image and declares that in Jeremiah 1:5 when he said, "Before I formed you in the womb, I knew you, before you were born, I set you apart; I appointed you as a prophet to the nations. This great proclamation by almighty God to Jeremiah is the same for all his people. He knew us before we were formed and wants to build a strong Nation as we reach for the living water of peace and grace.

How do we get that living water? There have been times in life that I had to break down the walls of unforgiveness that encumbered me. Pain that penetrated my soul left me hopeless wondering if God saw my pain. Each time I came to this crossroad in my life, the cross came to memory. The good thing is that Jesus never left me, he carried me through the tough times with tenderness and love. He had fresh water when I was thirsty and offered me living water that would flow within my soul breaking down condemnation and offering his peace.

God wants the walls that enslave this great country to fall. He made our Nation and offers his peace as we all take our differences and collaborate a healthy world through the living water of our Lord and savior. This is the time we need to work together as our country heals. Jesus offers living water for humanity that will be sustainable and bring healing during our nation's pandemic. God bless you this day as you serve him.

HEALING FOR AMERICA

2 CHRONICLES 7:14

If my people, who are called by my name, will humble themselves and pray and seek my face and turn from their wicked ways, then will I hear from heaven and will forgive their sins and will heal their land.

As I end this six-month devotional. I would like to share stories with you of answered prayer as I have made my journey. I am seventy-nine- and one-half years of age and when doubt comes, God takes me back to these moments of answered prayer.

When I was in my early twenties, I shared a home with a dear lady from Ukraine. The home had such an inviting aroma as she baked the apple strudel's, cherry strudel along with homemade bread daily. She would often come to the top of the steps calling out my name with a box filled with goodies for the day. As I peered into her eyes, I could see Jesus. I was sick with rheumatic fever and told I could never work again, nor could I have more children. At that time, I only had one child. During my helplessness I knelt to pray telling God that I needed a touch from the master's hand. During the summer I attended a church camp and was anointed by the dear saints of God and God miraculously healed me. This was my miracle from almighty God that is still fresh in my spirit to this day.

Our world needs prayer that God is so willing to give. 2 Chronicles 7:14 is a promise to his people. May we come together and humble ourselves seeking healing for America and our Nation.

ASK, SEEK, KNOCK

MATTHEW 7:7

Ask and it will be given to you, seek and you will find; knock and the door will be opened to you.

Parenting as biological parents is often synonymous with how God parents, we, his children. He evaluates the situation and then he answers according to what he wants to conduct in our lives. If the request is not selfish and brings about good, he will smile and grant our prayer request.

Many years ago, while in college, I was working full time and trying to complete my education. That particular quarter, I was taking law. During the evening before my exam, my body broke out in hives. It started from the neck to the feet. The itching was uncontrollable, and I did not know what I was going to do. I had an exam the next day and knew if I did not get relief, I would not be able to take that exam. The night had fallen, and it was nine PM. The scripture in Matthew 7:7 asks to seek, and knock came to mind. I opened my Bible to that scripture, placed my hands and said Lord this was your promise, so I am asking for you to remove these hives, so I rest and be able to take my exam tomorrow. Sometimes God answers prayers in his timing, however this time it was instant. The hives left and from that day forward I have never had it again. God cares about the trivial things in life because we are his children. I am glad I had that experience' because it lets me know what a great heavenly father I have. Out of my excitement, I showed my children God's grace and healing at a desperate moment.

America, God wants to parent his people. He wants to go to the White House bringing peace and hope to democracy as we walk through the challenging times.

AMERICA THE BEAUTIFUL

GENESIS 1:1

In the Beginning God created the heavens and the earth. The creation story shared by the word of God will forever live within our hearts.

In the early years growing up, as soon as we moved into an area my father would look for a church. My dad and my mother left a heritage within my life that will never go away. Each Sunday morning, we would sit at the table have our breakfast and then the night before we would lay out our clothes and pin curl our hair like they used to do in those days. We were getting ready for the celebration the next morning.

God created all things just for the liking of mankind. He pointed the world to strength and peace leaving out the chaotic mess that humanity can sometimes bring. His love reaches to the highest mountain and to the lowest valley that sin often brings. He formed within man a desire that can be fulfilled just for the asking. Never is our Lord obnoxious or crude he extends his hand of mercy for all who is willing to come. He is our lifeline to eternal peace and joy as we make our journey here on earth. He has designed a road map for us to follow so we do not step outside the boundaries of safety.

America, God is the same today yesterday and forever. He never changes. Throughout my life I have never forgotten how he took special time and showed me he is an everlasting and merciful God. I have never doubted one moment that healing is waiting for our great country. As we walk through these times together, let us hold on to his promises and to each other in dignity and respect. We are a family that is designed by Almighty God.

A PARENT'S MIRACLE

ACTS 4:12

Salvation is found in no one else, for there is no other name under heaven given to men by which we must be saved.

One of the greatest gifts we can give our children is teaching them about the life of our Savior. As hard as we might try, there are times that our children will stray away from their family heritage and faith.

When my daughter left home, she strayed from the Lord. As I approached her one day while sitting in the parking lot at Wendy's. She said, "Mommy, I cannot live that kind of life anymore because things are so different." I explained that salvation is a special gift and when we ask for forgiveness for our sins, we take the gift and let the Lord unwrap the gift daily as needed. We prayed the sinner's prayer that day and her life totally changed. Her life will live forever within those people that she touched daily. As a parent, that was my answered prayer that God would perform a miracle in her life. The difference between God and Man is God can change a heart and man cannot.

America, as we face tumultuous times, may we look past all the affirmations the world offers about where we live, where we work, level of education as an antidote for success. Salvation is such an effortless process that will forever change who you are and what you become. God wants to heal our people and our land. Let us never let circumstances deter our relationship with the Lord Jesus Christ. As I am sharing how God answered my prayers along the way, the challenging times that Covid has brought to America, will end as we his people pray. Challenges will become victories.

THE GREATEST MIRACLE IN HISTORY

JOHN 14:1-3

Do not let your hearts be troubled. Trust in God; trust also in me. In my father's house are many rooms; if it were not so, I would have told you. I am going there to prepare a place for you. And if I go and prepare a place for you, I will come back and take you to be with me that you also may be where I am.

As Jesus prepared for his death and resurrection, he pulled his disciples aside to bring comfort to their souls. Even today as I read the word about the death and resurrection, I cannot understand the scene of events that occurred just prior to his death. The disciples heard his words when he instructed them, however it did not take residence within their being. The mere thought of crucifixion was incomprehensible to the disciples. He was their Lord.

The greatest miracle ever taken place in history took place when Mary Magdalene went early on the first day of the week as darkness pierced the land. As she approached the tomb, she discovered that the stone had been removed from the entrance. She saw two angels in white sitting in the place where the body had been placed. The great commission of Mary Magdalene a woman with a past was now chosen to tell society that he had risen from the dead.

Jesus chose Mary Magdalene even though society considered her an outcast to the religious community. She was the first to get a glimpse of our risen Lord. The walls of guilt by association from her past fell as she leaped with Joy that her Lord had risen from the dead. That is the greatest Miracle in History and Mary was the one chosen to tell share the good news.

I CAME TO BRING HEALING TO THE SICK

LUKE 5:31

Jesus answered them, "It is not the healthy who needs a doctor, but the sick. I have not come to call the righteous, but sinners to repentance.

I can just see Jesus as he approached Levi the tax collector at his tax booth, he asks him to follow him, and Levi got up left his work and followed the Lord. Looking for and saving the lost was the commission that God sent his only son Jesus to a fallen world, aspiring to nurture the sick bringing healing to the world not just a select few.

The invitation was quite an honor for Levi known as Matthew to get a special invitation to follow Jesus without reservation. He left his place of work and followed the Lord. Levi not only left his place of employment he held a great banquet at his home for the Lord. The Pharisees and teachers of the law complained that Jesus was associating with people not of their own kind. I can just see Jesus, tenderly saying, I have not come to call the righteous, but the sinners to repentance.

Luke being a highly educated man wanted to make sure that the events that happened in his Lord's life was written in chronical order being the reason for the birth and death of Christ. Luke a great man of faith left instructions of simplicity for believers as they make their journey serving the Lord.

As we face the great pandemic, let us reach those that are weary and sick offering the gift of salvation. Let us reach beyond the segregation and political walls that has enslaved this great country that we live in. May we be a Levi stepping outside the walls that divide offering peace to a fallen world.

HELPING THE WEAK

Romans 15:1-2

We who are strong ought to bear with the failings of the weak and not to please ourselves. Each of us should please his neighbor for his good, to build him up.

As I am completing my 181-days devotional, my desire is that I can help someone along the way who is struggling. There may be a neighbor that needs encouragement that an inspirational card will lift their spirits for the day.

Social stigma can be an avenue that we work on as we walk through the tough times. May we not label a person by their color or gender with discriminatory behavior. Working together and bearing the burdens of others, will bring Joy in the midst of a world that is upside down.

A family in the church was facing much sickness and monetary loss. The funds to take care of the family was not available. As they entered the church you could see the stress upon mom and dad's face. This is what Romans 15:1-2 is speaking about. We can attribute in so many ways discretely as God leads. The church is the lifeline to humanity.

When we go through trials that Covid has brough to our country, if we work together aspiring to build the aspirations of others, God will be please and bless this great Nation that we live in.

Hope is what we Christians build our lives upon, and courage gives us the tenacity to complete and share with a world that is hurting.

WHERE DO WE GO FROM HERE AMERICA?

Proverbs 4:20-22

My son, pay attention to what I say; listen closely to my words, do not let them out of your sight, keep them within your heart; for they are life to those who find them and health to a man's whole body.

The word of God has always been a lifeline for me as I have made my journey through life raising my family, maneuvering through the work world, and working within the body of Christ. The bible speaks of the many miraculous healings that took place during the life of Christ and after his death.

If I take a special time of day to be alone in prayer with the Lord, I find that comfort and peace permeates my heart bringing strength to manage my day-to-day activities. The Lord's Prayer brings great comfort, especially the part that says Hallowed Be Thy Name, it is a form of praise, gratitude, and respect to our heavenly father.

It is so easy to get sidetrack in the busy world we live in. Everything is at such a fast pace and all too often our bible reading, and prayer life comes to a standstill. I do not think we do it intentionally, we just busy ourselves to the point that we forget that reading and praying is the lifeline to a successful Christian life.

I mentioned to you in the second reading about the Butterfly with a broken wing, America our wings have been clipped and God will restore our brokenness financially and spiritually as we listen to the instruction of King Solomon.

Learning to take spiritual instructions can be hard but the results is phenomenal. God Bless you and this great Nation that we live in.

I KNOW HIM, I CAN FEEL HIM, I CAN SEE HIM

ISAIAH 30:20-21

And though the Lord gives you the bread of adversity and the water of affliction, yet your teacher will not hide himself anymore, but your eyes shall see your teacher and your ears shall hear a word behind you, say, this is the way, walk in it, when you turn to the right or to the left.

As I close this last devotion, my purpose is to show you that we as Americans serve a wonderful Lord and Savior that will answer prayer in methods that we often do not understand. I do not understand how God performed the miracles in my own life, but I do know that he loved me so much that he gave me my special time with him that no one can take away. My healing from Rheumatic Fever was a miracle. The revelation of his presence with the paint bucket for a teenager. Parkers fish story was a moment he appeared when we prayed for a fish, he gave Parker many fish. Notoriety was just for Parker, Lana, and me. I loved this moment when God made his presence known.

As I look out over our universe, I can see God's careful planning as he placed our world into existence. The amazement of nature has always permeated my mind. He gave us such a beautiful garden of hope and peace as we serve him. I can see him in a child, I can see his handiwork when he changes a sinful heart to a heart of peace.

The song, God Bless America brings a tear to my eyes whenever I hear it. May we always give back to our maker that part of our lives that will make America strong. When we include the Lord in our decisions, he will bring strength and power to America. He who dwells in the shelter of the highest will rest in the shadow of the almighty.

ABOUT THE AUTHOR

At the age of thirteen, I accepted the Lord as my personal Savior. The transformation took place in a small church in Elyria, OH. As I knelt at the altar, there seem to be a tugging in my heart that took me back to the first scripture I learned as a four-year-old. The Lord is My Shepherd, I shall not want.

I married at the age of twenty and God gave me three precious children. Alcohol and infidelity brought the marriage to a close leaving me unequipped as I was not the most studious student in high school. Situations in life forced me to enroll at Lorain County Community College. As I enrolled, fear of failure played over and over in my mind saying that college was not an option. Doors of opportunity opened for me as I put the negative thoughts out of my mind. I soon graduated with honors. (The Lord is My Shepherd; I shall not want.) This verse opened doors of success as I leaned on him during challenging times. I continued my education at Ashland University.

It is my desire to make a difference in the lives daily that I interact with sharing my own experiences to bring hope to those that face insurmountable circumstances. The Lord is My Shepherd walked me through divorce and the loss of two children. The Joy that God brings to one's life is an inward joy that supersede circumstances. 1 Thessalonians 5:16 Be joyful always.

Leda Rafter

www.ingramcontent.com/pod-product-compliance
Ingram Content Group UK Ltd.
Pitfield, Milton Keynes, MK11 3LW, UK
UKHW041953230426
12048UKWH00008B/306